Living the INNERGIZED Life

Transforming Ordinary Moments into Extra-Ordinary Memories

Compilation by Cathy L. Davis

Living the Innergized Life
Transforming Ordinary Moments into Extra-Ordinary Memories

Published by **UpsiDaisy Press**, St. Louis, MO
Copyright ©2017 Cathy L. Davis
All rights reserved.

No part of this publication may be reproduced, stored in a retrieval system, or transmitted in any form or by any means, electronic, mechanical, photocopying, recording, scanning, or otherwise, except as permitted under Section 107 or 108 of the 1976 United States Copyright Act, without the prior written permission of the Publisher. Requests to the Publisher for permission should be addressed to Cathy@daviscreative.com, please put **INNERGIZED LIFE** in the subject line.

Limit of Liability/Disclaimer of Warranty: While the publisher and authors have used their best efforts in preparing this book, they make no representations or warranties with respect to the accuracy or completeness of the contents of this book and specifically disclaim any implied warranties of appropriateness or merchantability for a particular purpose. The advice and strategies contained herein may not be suitable for your situation. You should consult with a professional where appropriate. Neither the publisher nor author shall be liable for any loss of profit or any other commercial damages, including but not limited to special, incidental, consequential, or other damages.

All contributing authors to this anthology have submitted their chapters to an editing process, and have accepted the recommendations of the editors at their own discretion. All authors have approved their chapters prior to publication.

Cover photo: Lonnie Gatlin

Cover and Interior design: DavisCreative.com

Editor: Pam Wilson

Living the Innergized Life
ISBN: 978-09774886-1-2

For the Team:

The Dreamers and Schemers,

The Believers and Conceivers.

Table of Contents

Cathy Davis
Raise Your Voice... 1

Carol Scott
Becoming My S.E.L.F. 7

Brenda Fraser
Plant the End Result Firmly in Mind 13

Laurie Ritchie
Revealing Our Inner Master "PEACE" 19

Dr. Jayne Gardner
The Divine Intelligence Process.................................. 25

Melissa Nickelson
Live YOUR Life... 31

Marilyn Eagen
Follow Your Heart, Your Divine Inside.......................... 37

Gail Gates
Agingschmaging 43

Shannon Schindler Redman
Empowering YOU to Know Your Own Greatness.................. 49

Lisa Hautly
A Matter of Wellness 55

Theresa Jeevanjee
See What Love Can Do 61

Continued...

Cathy Sexton
Turning Bombshells Into Blessings 67

Dr. Julie Steinhauer
Vision for Life 73

Karen O. Drake
Finding Life's Balance 79

Beth Hammock
Bliss on the Go 85

Jeannie Krause-Taylor
"Like Mother, Like Daughter" 91

Kelly DeRossett
A Blank Canvas 97

Pat Powers
Finding My Inner Child 103

Pam Wilson
The Story Teller 109

Rev. Denise Judd
Unlocking the Heart 115

CATHY DAVIS

Raise Your Voice

If you grew up reading Dr. Seuss, you are probably quite familiar with "Horton Hears a Who" (originally published August 12, 1954), the metaphorical story of many tiny voices joining together in a chorus loud enough to be heard. The story resonated with me as a child, and seems to be an appropriate metaphor for the state of our planet lately.

Just as in the Dr. Seuss book, if you listen to ANY news program recently, you hear many voices throughout the world simultaneously asking to be heard. Voices shouting of decades and generations—if not centuries—of persecution based upon race, color, gender, nationality, physical or mental abilities, sexual orientation, religion, family culture or politics… and more. Many voices, joining in chorus, to find a better way of living, loving and learning to co-exist.

As a young, white female growing up in mid-America, my complaints were minimal—middle class, public schools, and my mother loved to buy me clothes. I lived with my mother and stepfather; my sister and brother were 12 and 10 years older, respectively, and had already moved out on their own. My parents had their own struggles, addictions and aggravations, so we ended up moving around a lot—I think mostly because they kept trying to flee their own struggles. In the midst of all the chaos, I was learning to form my own opinions and how to voice them.

I can still remember the exact day when someone tried to tell me my voice did not count—third grade, just before dinner. I don't recall the subject of the conversation, but I vaguely remember my stepfather asking me to do something (probably set the table or such). My independent 8-year-old-self told him, "No thank you, I'm busy." At which point, my mother explained I was not allowed to tell an adult, "No," let alone a MALE adult. Now, granted, this was early 1960s, and the most popular show on TV was "Father Knows Best."

I remember feeling confused, yet based upon the tone of my mother's voice, knew I definitely needed to follow her lead in order to stay safe. I felt silenced, discounted, and little... and although I did not know the word when I was 8, I felt BE-littled. It wasn't until recently (when the "me too" campaign came to light) that this memory came full-circle, and I began to realize how much of an impact that one conversation has had on every male relationship I've had over the past 50-plus years.

A voice waiting to be heard.

I now see how that first incident, with my mother and stepfather, fueled my determination to raise my voice. As I grew older, I became the over-achiever, determined to prove my worth. In grade school, I was the kid who raised her hand first; I was compelled to make sure people understood that I knew things and my opinion mattered. In junior high, I was the helper and the organizer, always helping with extra-curricular and volunteer activities. As I entered high school in the mid-1970s, I began to see a subtle change in how females were perceived, when two male teachers became my cheerleaders. My art teacher noticed I had an affinity for drawing, and went out of his way to talk the school into bending the rules so I could enroll in the beginning Drafting Class—to see if I might want a career in architecture or the graphic arts. As the first female in the all-male class, I got a lot of attention—not only from my male class mates, but, more importantly to me, from the male teacher. I think he enjoyed having someone in class who was not just there for the class credit. Under the tutelage of two open-minded male teachers, my passion for drawing took off and paved the way for my future career.

Looking back, I was never one to silence my opinion, yet, many times I was hushed, or I hushed myself, and fell silent to better fit in with societal expectations. I'd voice my opinions in private, becoming even more brave and opinionated as I entered college. I was beginning to better understand why I had a need to offer my opinions and prove my value. In my heart, I knew my voice mattered—even as I was still learning to define what my opinions were.

A voice learning to be heard.

As I entered the corporate workforce in the early 1990s, I landed in the predominantly male-driven world of financial services. I learned the subtle nuances of wearing a bright red suit when invited to join a meeting full of male counterparts. I learned to use the "Wonder Woman" stand when speaking, and I learned to never stand behind the podium, as it always made me look shorter than I really was. There was no class offered to learn these things—as a female, we learned these strategies from watching those females on the ladder above us. After 12 years of marketing financial services, and having experienced two downsizings, I took a leap of faith and started my own brand consulting business in 2004. Ready, or not, I was stepping onto the path of entrepreneurship, and, through real-life experiences, would be learning how to take my voice to the next level.

Looking back, I see how my personal path has always been about ME finding my voice, and more recently, about helping others to find and express their voices. For the past 14 years, I've been helping small businesses and entrepreneurs find their Brand Voice, and 12 years ago, we began helping our clients express their voices even more, through the world of publishing (it was 2005 when we first helped a client publish their book).

I now recognize my current voice originated from that little conversation my mother had with me when I was in third grade, and my quiet non-agreement to not be silenced. My voice now fuels my passion to help others find their voice and tell their story.

That's what this book is all about.

The "*Living the INNERGIZED Life*" anthology is a compilation of stories shared by women who have found their voice and are ready to be heard. These stories we share are written by women who have found a way to transcend the craziness of day-to-day living, choosing to navigate life by connecting to what they define as their Higher Power, Inner Knowing or God-Source—that One Still Voice. It's not about one particular belief system or particular religion, but rather about how their inner guidance system, uniquely defined by each woman, becomes their own individual source of undeniable INNER ENERGY… allowing them to function at a much higher, INNERGIZED level on a daily basis. Join us as we learn from their experiences, and feel free to reach out to any of them to continue the conversation. You'll find their contact information at the end of each of their chapters.

Is your voice ready to be heard?

Everyone has a story, and many have stories which need to be told. You, too, probably have at least one story to tell. Over the years, we've identified three main types of stories in the hundreds of non-fiction books we've published. As you read the stories in this book, you may recognize these themes…

- **Struggle Story:** all about turning your life's MESS into a re-solution MESSAGE to help others step out of their own struggle
- **Soapbox Story:** this version demonstrates your expert knowledge and offers a new perspective for your reader, in support of a cause or movement
- **System Story:** a step-by-step systematic process, offering hope and relief to readers who want to learn how to do something

As Professional Author Consultants, we help you tell your story, no matter where you are in the process of writing your book—from simply having an "idea" about a book, all the way to the other end of the spectrum, when you may have your book completely written. Our highly-experienced editors and writing coaches help you become authors and our publishing consultants teach you how to be your own publisher—you get to avoid the self-publishing pitfalls, and keep 100% of your royalties.

Recently, one of our clients introduced me as her "Publishing Doula." I pretty much hold your hand, walk you through the process, and guarantee a pain-free delivery of your book to your doorstep and out into the world.

Really. It's much easier than childbirth.

I hope you enjoy our stories…

Cathy Davis is the CEO of Davis Creative, a branding services agency headquartered in St Louis, MO, specializing in brand strategy, graphic design and independent publishing. With clients in all 50 states, Davis Creative is known for helping purpose-driven clients Look Good, Attract More Clients and Monetize Their Passion.

The bulk of Cathy's professional career was at Bank of America (formerly NationsBank, Boatmen's) marketing trust services to high-net-worth clients. After several mergers and 2 downsizings, she founded Davis Creative, LLC in January of 2004. Her husband, Jack joined her the Summer of 2008, after nearly 20 years at Fleishman-Hillard public relations.

As a professional branding and author consultant, books and publishing have always been an integral part of Cathy's life—from making them as a student in college, to working for a major book retailer after college, to collecting them for her personal library. A former board member of the St. Louis Publisher's Association, she began introducing her clients to the power of self-publishing in 2005.

Cathy L. Davis
888-598-0886
cathy@DavisCreative.com
www.DavisCreative.com

www.facebook.com/DavisCreativeLLC/
www.linkedin.com/in/cathyldavis/

CAROL SCOTT

Becoming My S.E.L.F.

My big dream is to improve the treatment of children in America, and I achieve my dream by helping YOU. Through my classes and consultation, as you create relationships that satisfy, fulfill, and uplift you, you coincidentally develop the ability to see children differently…and, I hope, a desire to treat them differently.

As my personal dream incubated vehicles to make your life better, my INNERgized life was born. Three life moments created this mission and, ultimately, the *7 Childhood Treasures* and *7 Facets of Team Success*, my tools to raise productivity and joy in your life. First I saw the nature of God, then the origins of human potential, and finally my own healing soul. These three extraordinary outcomes arose from three perfectly ordinary moments.

Each turning point truly seemed a humdrum activity. Gazing down from an airplane at 16, I suddenly, simply *knew* that we are all One. At 18, choosing college courses, the advisor said, "Lots of students like 'Introduction to Child Development.' It's self-paced." My immediate "Yay!-Easy-A!" reaction launched my lifelong journey to learn how we are shaped by early development and what we can do about it. At 30, waking from yet another night of partying, I heard a voice within whisper, "Is there something wrong with getting high every day…?" This simple question led me to therapy, sobriety, and recovery from 14 years of my father's sexual assaults.

By a grander plan than mine, these early-planted seeds were gestating to someday yield fruit as classes and consultation on the *7 Childhood Treasures* and the *7 Facets of Team Success*. From 18 to 25, knowledge about children's development poured into me as light into a hungry darkness. Then, I had to get out of my own way; stop letting the wounds of my childhood drive my life. I had to stop self-medicating my pain, to let the light of my Innergy shine! Before I could truly thrive, I had to become my **Self**-governing, **E**go-aware, **L**eading, **F**ree **S.E.L.F.**, concepts that are tenets of my empowering programs for your growth.

I began my child development career but, sadly, my personal life was in chaos. I drank too much on too many nights. Romantic and sexual relationships were short-lived and dysfunctional; married at 22 and divorced at 25. My unrestrained behavior created ridiculous risks. At 25 and just starting that first "real" job, I didn't expect to live to age 30.

In hindsight, I was "acting out" a subconscious wish to escape childhood trauma buried deeply in my body and my dreams, both of which I self-medicated into oblivion. Committing a form of slow suicide by addiction, I subconsciously wished for a sudden accident to free me. My faith, still solitary and undeveloped, provided little balance for my fatalism.

If you'd met me then, you'd have seen my little life car was driven by all the deadly sins at once, full throttle, up on two wheels for every curve. Beneath the wild surface, lived a deep void of "wrongness." My nimble intellect tried to compensate for my lack of social and emotional intelligence but I felt out of place, out of step, outside of an understanding everyone else seemed to share.

Then, I turned 30, and along came the third ordinary moment; waking the morning after my birthday party, wondering whether using drugs and alcohol every day was a problem. By then, I was a young, published professional, a couple of years into a PhD program. With responsibility for a preschool and its undergrad and grad student staff, I was an "up and coming" professional. My outward veneer impeccable; my personal chaos contained.

I emphasize these circumstances because in hindsight it does seem odd that the question, "Is something wrong here?" had not occurred before. But using every day was just what I did, and had done for more than a decade. Getting drunk whenever I drank just seemed normal, because everybody I knew did that. Binge eating, serial monogamy of dysfunctional relationships, living with big drama between me and my friends and family, and hiding all this craziness at work? That was just life.

Suddenly, then, there was this question, hanging. What if this life was *not* normal?

That thought in my waking mind hid that INNERgizing pivot, landing me in desperately-needed therapy. Only later did I understand that on this journey *I had a unique advantage*. My healing and growth were exponentially enhanced by my knowledge of child development and my faith, which created the readiness to heal.

When I remembered my early traumas, I understood them deeply, *from the perspective of the child I was* because, as a researcher studying child development and a professional working directly with children, I knew children. As my therapists helped me understand adult relationships, I watched children daily develop relationships in the social laboratory of preschool. I noticed that therapy encouraged the same capacities that preschoolers learned: trust, emotional intelligence, intention. I was on their natural developmental pathway…but from ages 33 to 44, rather than from 3 to 4.

At first, that wealth of enhanced understanding was all for me. Eventually, my growth led me to share my experience with others. I began to see Divine purpose in my life of "chaos," as I found spiritual communities in which to develop my faith. Exposure to meditation, earth-based spirituality, ecstatic music, mythology, and affirmative prayer fortified that faith.

Pow! My INNERgized life was born, and I began teaching others how *their* early child development affected *their* lives. I created the **7 Childhood Treasures** and **7 Facets of Team Success**, and from early workshop groups, I learned that my frameworks also helped those who were never abused. The vision crystallized fully when I realized that developmental assets from the early years are *often* left behind, even when parents do a pretty good job.

Those who have experienced my classes and consultation over a dozen years can testify: when you understand how *your* early development affected *your* life, you revise every relationship. Why? Because knowing how an infant learns to trust, you better understand how stronger trust can fortify your marriage or your work team. When you understand how toddlers find healthy boundaries, you strengthen your own independence.

The **7 Treasures** or **7 Facets** work leads to profoundly deep change, forgiveness, and inspiring dreams. They allow you to actively pursue your INNERgized life. As I continue my own personal transformation, sharing in the work with you, you feel safe to uncover your vulnerability and grow with me.

Regardless of your childhood's blessings or tragedies, knowing how your development was *supposed* to go in those first seven years will change your life, as it changed hundreds. Observing you apply what I teach is the spiritual fuel that keeps me INNERgetically reaching for my life mission. Remember, that big dream is *To Improve the Treatment of Children in America*. And you can help!

The 7 Childhood Treasures and **7 Facets of Team Success** are for you, for your growth. Drop the magnifying lens of personal transformation in favor of a kaleidoscope. After you see your life through the colorful lens of your first seven years, you will see a different you. An added benefit, and my secret strategy to further my life mission, is that you will also never again see young children in the same way.

With my S.E.L.F.—**S**elf-governed, **E**go-aware, and **L**eading my life, **F**ree of self-imposed barriers—I foster your healthy capacities for Trust, Independence, Faith, Negotiation, Vision, Compromise, and Acceptance. With these gemstones filling the treasure chest of your spirit, you become your S.E.L.F., too. My bonus is that you'll also be more respectful of both the vulnerabilities and the potential of babies, toddlers and preschoolers.

And that kaleidoscope view of them is not only good for the children; it's good for all of us.

L. Carol Scott, PhD discovered the power of the **7 Treasures** during her own recovery from years of childhood sexual assault. Then she discovered that this methodology based on early childhood development was beneficial to everyone—not just those with dysfunctional childhoods.

Carol traversed her early years with one parent an alcoholic sociopath, and the other struggling to cope using a very lean toolbox of skills for marriage and parenting. Carol's first seven years, and the adolescence that followed, left her standing at the threshold to adulthood with no tools at all for coping with adult relationships. Her road to recovery included many years of psychotherapy and deep introspection.

Carol's successful career focuses on early childhood development and its impact on adults. For more than four decades, she has worked directly with thousands of children and adults, from the various perspectives of teacher, teacher educator, program director or agency CEO, presenter/trainer, and consultant. Her education includes:

- BA in Human Development and Family Life
- BA in Anthropology
- MA in Early Childhood Education
- PhD in Developmental and Child Psychology

At the intersection of her personal experience and professional insights about the first seven years of life, Carol found strategies that enable you to refresh, renew, resuscitate, and even revive your relationships and interactions, at home and at work.

Continued…

- **The 7 Childhood Treasures** add impact as you learn and evolve as a person.
- **The 7 Facets of Team Success** bring personal power and perspective to your career and workplace.

From a refreshing retreat for a workplace team, to a major overhaul of corporate culture, the **7 Facets** bring a uniquely productive lens to business. For individuals in any stage of therapy, recovery, spiritual seeking, or other transformational journey, seeing life from the perspective of the **7 Treasures** allows you to take your relationships and your life to the next level, and leave the struggle behind.

L. Carol Scott, PhD
866-665-5569
carol@LCarolScott.com
www.LCarolScott.com

www.facebook.com/Dr.L.CarolScott
www.linkedin.com/in/carol-scott-7b70429/
@LCarolScott on Twitter

PO Box 1122
Maryland Heights, MO, 63043

BRENDA FRASER

Plant the End Result Firmly in Mind

"When the end result is planted firmly in your mind, then all the necessary steps will open up to you."

Rev. Dr. Lawrence De Rusha

What is your "end result"? What is the thing you have been "meaning to do" for years? The thing on your bucket list you must do before you die? THAT thing, is the thing I encourage you to dream about, pray about, and start working towards. "Someday" never comes unless you take steps, and actions to manifest the dream.

My big dream was to travel to Africa "someday." Not just any part of Africa, but Ghana specifically. It's on the Western coast, and has a long and rich history, from hundreds of years of the Gold trade giving it the name "the Gold Coast", and later a tragic history with African slave trading. One small area in eastern Ghana is known as the Krobo region, and it is in this specific region, that recycled glass beads have been made for more than 500 years.

Traditionally, Krobo beads were made by only men over an open fire with excessive high heat. The glass beads are hand-painted by artists, each artist marking the beads with their own designs. The beads were hand strung by women into necklaces and earrings. In recent years, the beads have been exported and sold internationally. Prized among jewelry designers worldwide, the beads historically were worn in ceremonies such as "Dipo" which is the coming-of-age ceremony indicating that a woman is "ready to be married", and has learned all the necessary skills to be a good wife. These ceremonies still continue, but the beads are also sold for every day jewelry designs, both in the local farmers markets in Ghana, and exported by a variety of businesses.

I had first heard about Ghana from one of my sisters who lived there in the late 60s and early 70s with her young family, having moved there for her husband's job. She gave birth to a child or two in Ghana. She and her family would visit my mother and me, exposing me, a child of 9 or 10 years old, to the traditional folk crafts of Africa. Growing up in a conservative, non-diverse area of New England, very Catholic and very homogeneous, I was always curious about African culture, and later in life, the bead-making and jewelry-making.

I saved up my money for almost a full year and raised some on sites like GoFundMe.Com. Before leaving, I asked Rev. Dr. Lawrence De Rusha of the Center for Spiritual Living in St. Louis for a "Travel Blessing." He suggested whenever I felt alone or scared, to put my hand over my heart, imagine a safe temple, and mentally "go to that safe spot within." I also learned a mantra, such as "I am safe. I am loved. I am protected."

We always have the choice to go within to find safety and love. Regardless of the outward appearance of chaos or drama, we can choose to go to that inside temple of timeless love.

My faith was tested in Africa one hallowed eve.

It was the week before Halloween in the United States, but in the Krobo district of Ghana, it was the annual Ngmayem festival, a week-long celebration of the harvest. The 13 regional chiefs are traditionally honored, carried around on elevated platforms, shaded with crimson red umbrellas. The tradition is to bring them bottles of gin, dance in the streets, and enjoy the ceremonial dances of the young Dipo girls wearing dozens of strands of heavy glass beads. The elder women dance too in a courtyard. At one event, I sat with the chief's wife (a.k.a. "the Queen Mother"), and her mother, as well as several "sub-chiefs". They wore traditional garments, carried golden staffs, and someone sprinkled millet seeds in my lap for "luck." I took hours and hours of video and photos at two different events. I danced in the streets waving a piece of white cloth to celebrate "victory." It was an amazing cultural experience and I soaked in every moment, waving to the little children, all of them staring at me because of my white-white skin and blond hair.

Each night, upon returning to my locally-based housing (not a hotel or guarded location), I put my hand over my heart, said my mantra, and tried to fall asleep. I slept in a nightshirt with only a small sheet, underneath a baby blue mosquito net.

On the last day of festival week, people from all over come to town, and just like Mardi Gras in New Orleans, the streets are full of revelry, drinking and festivities.

In the middle of the night around 2 am, I awoke to what appeared to be a nightmare coming true. Three men were grabbing my arms, and tying me up. They pulled down the baby blue mosquito net and used it to gag me, and demanded, "Where's the cash?!" as they started tearing through my suitcase, flipping my bedding, and looking in every nook and cranny for cash.

One of the three threw me to the cement floor and sat atop me while the others continued to search for piles of money they believed I had hidden as most Americans do carry cash with them. I closed my eyes, remaining passive and quiet on the floor, as it was becoming all too real that they could easily kill me. Using visualization techniques, I imagined myself surrounded in white light…I imagined my mother in Heaven and my angel I call "Amelia" (after aviator Earhart). I imagined my safety, I imagined my mother's love, I imagined love all around me, and not the unfolding chaos. As fast as they arrived, the men fled without raping me or killing me. They did however, shove their dirty thumbs down my throat to damage my vocal chords, and prevent me from screaming for help right away. I thought I would pass out and die from the choking, but thankfully, they stopped a millisecond before I went unconscious.

As I've been taught over the years, I relied on the Invisible Power within me to survive a situation most would think would be impossible. As Rev. Larry said recently, and I paraphrase, "If you find yourself at the edge of fear, and you drop it and surrender, you will experience a transformation like never before." You can challenge yourself and push on. When your mind tells you NO, and screams it at you, you can still push on, if you rely on your inner power, your inner source of love, he said.

If I had known I would be attacked, would I have gone to Africa? The answer is unequivocally, "yes." I went not only to experience the local culture and learn new things about another part of the world, but I also went to help and be of service. I went to meet some of the local women, and inspire them about the larger world that exists outside their village. I have always enjoyed empowering women to dream and to grow. I wasn't going for only myself, I was going with a purpose and a mission.

I have the good feeling of knowing I touched the lives of many women that I met while there, the jewelry designers, and some of the bead sellers from the market. I worked with several women in their 20s and 30s teaching them computer skills and how to type their name. Most of the women had never sat at a computer keyboard. I gave them hope, I inspired them. I encouraged many to return to school and continue their education.

A month after my return, I received a box with thank-you notes taped to the backside of their photos—photos in which they wore the necklaces and earrings I designed for them individually while over there. Perhaps one or two of them will pursue further education…maybe one or two might leave their village someday and travel to America…maybe one or two might realize they too have inner resources of power and love that can surmount any situation.

My hope for you, the reader, is that you challenge yourself to pursue something on your bucket list. Surround yourself with people like the other authors in this book and women in your community who will say YES to your dreams. Don't let fear stop you from doing the outrageous thing you think you cannot do by yourself. This is your life, your journey, and you will experience a transformation if you release your fear, rely on a mantra or prayer, trust that there is a protective source watching over you and guiding you. No matter what—you are safe and you are loved. You will be blessed as you serve others. Love IS all around..

Brenda Fraser: Plant the End Result Firmly in Mind

Brenda A. Fraser is a jewelry designer and owner of "Butterfly & Moon", a women's fashion and jewelry boutique in historic Saint Charles, MO. She makes jewelry with beads from Africa, Australia, and other places she has visited. She is also known as a mosaic artist, using vintage jewelry pieces to create uplifting works of art on metal and wood. She hosted "Alive to Thrive" for 5+ years on Blogtalk Radio.

Brenda is a member of Zonta International and a Past Club President. She was a Beyond the Best winner named by *Streetscape Magazine*. Brenda serves as Deputy Treasurer for a Missouri State Senate campaign, www.BillingsforSenate.com. butterflyandmoon.com, ButterflyandMoon@gmail.com

Brenda Fraser
636-493-1121
ButterflyandMoon@gmail.com
www.ButterflyandMoon.com

www.Facebook.com/ButterflyandMoon
@butterflynmoon
@galaforcellc

Butterfly & Moon
814 South Main St
St Charles, MO 63301

LAURIE RITCHIE

Revealing Our Inner Master "PEACE"

Creative expression is dying inside you.

Dying because of the voices in your head that you know well: "I'm not creative enough, wealthy enough, thin enough, smart enough, well read, well travelled, well connected, too old…" I'm just not ENOUGH to do what I really want! You've been listening to all the opinions around you that affirm your supposed short-comings, sending you on a rat wheel of others' and possibly your own, though mostly subconscious, hoops to jump through.

And that's killing your creative expression. Can you see how it would? Creative expression is the playful, inner child of wonder, acceptance and love; she exists in the mystery, the inner UNIQUENESS of your Being. Creative expression is possibility, exploration, trust, play, flow!

What if our "creative expression" dies?

Because YOU die too. A little piece of you dies every day until you're just the human shell, acting as a puppet of expectations, without your vibrant soul. You lose the inner spark that makes you sing, that joins hands with the Energy of the world that creates hope, joy, and wonder of all that is. You drown in depression, anxiety, addiction, fatigue, illness, and anger.

I was a child of imagination and whimsy; I loved catching fireflies, lighting my nightstand in a jar. Joining my parents, cradled in a canoe of adventure with all our camping supplies. Dreaming up dress designs for hours with my girl friends out of a simple towel. My nose always stuck in a book. Doing every possible craft kit known to woman or child.

Around eight or nine, that child self begins to listen to the outer world. It's when we start buying into the notion that the "fluff of life", those external factors such as money, popularity, getting ahead, being a "good/nice" girl become more important. It feels as though we'd better crack the whip so we don't get left behind. Competition, fitting in, appearance, popularity, and having stuff is the name of the game as piece by piece, we begin to hide away those creative, unique traits and dreams.

My family, perhaps like every other well meaning American family, taught me with a strong voice of opinion about what was right. They pushed me to reach my ultimate best. My upper middle class experience led me towards a practical occupation, a husband that would keep me financially secure. I dumbed down my inner creative, possibly "wacky" intuitive life and followed the rules.

I did all the "right" things: all the measures of success that were expected of me I completed. I was a good follower, a do-gooder! And though I don't regret any of this, there was an inner spark of Laurie directed "creative" flow that was missing. A quirky, imaginative, creative self that wasn't always directed or "reasonable". It wasn't until I'd checked all the boxes of college, career, marriage, children, involved motherhood, that I began to wonder where the hell "me" went. When things started venturing south as I created a secretive life for myself that was filled with shame, anger, and lack of integrity, I lifted my head and wondered, "How the hell did I get here? Who is this person? And why??"

Expressive Arts showed up coincidentally on my computer screen when I began Googling what I really wanted to be when I grew up. It was a nice mix of what I loved in my chosen field of mental health Occupational Therapy and my love of all things Art. I sent an email to ask about the certification program in New York, facing down all my fears of not being ready or smart or creative enough, and found that there was ONE spot left open. It began the following month. No time to self-doubt: another favorite past-time. I remember waking up that first morning in the hotel room in New York and feeling as if I was waking up to My True Life for the first time. As I went through the program, I remember my inner child/expressiveness went wild, keeping me awake at night as she danced with ideas and ecstatic joy. I offer my forgiveness now for the long emails I shared with the instructors that first weekend, my inner child on fire as I shared every nuance of glee in connection back to my Heart with another human being!

Early on in my Expressive Art journey I created an artwork that expresses my philosophical belief about our human existence. In my childlike love of color,

I heaped an entire spectrum together in a finger painting. As the colors became muddy and black, I became frustrated. I then scraped off this excess only to reveal the vibrancy of all the colors below, embedded in the paper. This was a huge metaphor for me, revealing philosophically in a dramatic visual what I wholeheartedly believe.

We most certainly are this vibrant, magnificent array of color and beauty in our core—it is the heaping of all the external "crap" that we mix up that creates the black muck in our head. The muck is what causes us to act "badly". Even the worst of us are not "bad people"; we're just covered in the muck of life, some of us more than others. We all need tools to uncover that beautiful magnificence that exists beneath it. There are so many tools available to us that "scrape off the muck"; learning the language of metaphor through Art is just one. All of them exist in getting out of our critical, left brain mind. Right brained wisdom is a practice of getting quiet enough to hear the inner voice. And then, practice, study, explore it as if your life depended on it. Because it does.

I believe that art, all art; dance, visual arts, writing, music, drama, is the voice of Spirit—a Divine Energy that exists around us and within; it is a metaphor for what is happening in our lives. When we come to the blank page, we feel the same anxiety that we feel upon a new change in life. As we learn to simply dive into that anxiety, letting go of the outcome of being "good/bad" or "accomplished/child-like", we begin to learn the nudges from our gut that guides our next step.

The Art Making piece in Whole Arts is a lesson of listening to body or gut nudges and acting upon them with creative selection. For instance, close your eyes and listen to the gentle notes of a song, letting your body sway, only moving a body part when it feels guided to do so. In the same way, shut your eyes before the blank page, letting your arm/paintbrush dance on the paper, waiting for your gut to tell you to change motion or color. Letting go to take action in our body is the same on a painted page and as it is in our lives. Learning how that feels first in our gut, then in various creative endeavors, then in our lives is the practice of Inner Child and right brained wisdom or flow. As we learn to feel in our body and create in some way every day, we begin to flow in that infinity motion, dipping into creative Mystery: to listen, inspire, admire, gain clarity, and then act outward in creative flow to take action towards our Life's Purpose.

After art making, there's a time for quiet reflection, to sit with the now "Sacred Other" and allow our intuitive skills to develop and strengthen. The creation has something to say. It is NOT us; it is one with Spirit and speaks with direction, love, clarity. It is a practice to discern the critical voice of ego ("that painting is awful") to what Higher Wisdom may be saying. It involves quiet and tools that I teach in Whole Arts.

Today, I spend time daily in what the world might call "frivolous" or "luxury". I play in paint, writing, dance and nature and teach others to do the same. I offer a playful, meaningful space for groups and individuals to develop their own creative practice so that they strengthen their intuitive, creative muscle. They learn to battle fear and self-judgment, face their shadow, bringing new awareness to their life. The creative practice creates a sense of freedom as it opens possibilities and allows them to see situations in a new light. It re-connects them to incredible joy as they play in an arena of no right or wrong. It pushes them beyond their "reasonable" mind to suggest a new reality they'd never considered. It offers depth of understanding and continued inspiration to keep striving beyond the Dream.

Simply said, it truly reveals our magnificent Inner MasterPEACE.

Let it Be
Your creative practice doesn't have
to look like a gallery masterpiece,
It doesn't even have to be a
high school art student's prize.
Let it be the touch of your inner child,
the sinking in to peace
that exists in the musty, cool paint,
the messy question when colored pencil
meets the blank paper.
Let it be the silence and whisper
that enters through the cells of
your heart in a silent
conversation with the
Spritual Wholeness of your Being,
calling you back Alive.
–Laurie Ritchie
3.19.17

Laurie Ritchie: Revealing Our Inner Master "PEACE"

Laurie Ritchie is a certified expressive art facilitator, intuitive practitioner and graduate from the Ohio State University in occupational therapy, specializing in mental health. She created her business, **Whole Arts Connection**, for the purpose of awakening others to their highest potential through re-connecting with their soul-driven creative energies. She believes in the transformative power of all the arts, allowing imagination, play and discovery to illuminate new perspectives not found through critical, analytical thinking. She specializes in life changes due to health, addiction, aging, grief/death for youth and adults. She is a spiritual seeker, writer, visual artist, gym rat, outdoor and adventure enthusiast, and play addict.

Join Laurie for **Co-Create**: a once-monthly, intention-themed, drop-in-basis Expressive Art Night, providing an opportunity to infuse a taste of Expressive Arts into your life, offering a bit of inspiration and awareness. Enjoy two hours of creative energy to instill quiet musing/listening, joy, exploration, and innovativeness. Or get in contact with her to schedule a session for your friends, co-workers, or family at a location of your choosing. For more in-depth personal work, transformational 1:1 sessions are available.

Laurie Ritchie
314-915-0081
Laurie@WholeArtsConnection.com
www.WholeArtsConnection.com

www.facebook.com/wholeartsconnection
https://twitter.com/WholeArts

DR. JAYNE GARDNER

The Divine Intelligence Process

We are all divine.

This realization changed my life, and it will change yours: The source of all power lies within us. When we look within ourselves and accept that one truth, we can begin to create the limitless life we were meant to live. Awakening this divinity will change the way you see yourself; activating this divinity will change the way you view and create your world.

As a doctor of philosophy in counseling psychology, I have devoted the past three decades to the spiritual development of myself and others. Throughout my career as a psychotherapist, teacher, and spiritual life coach, I have witnessed amazing transformations that brought about a new or renewed sense of purpose and fulfillment. But that was not all. As people of all religious or non-religious backgrounds set off on their search for 'self' and changed their relationship with their self, they reported that their relationship with God had also evolved to a higher level; they began to connect with God in a new way.

I term the inherent, unlimited mindset "Divine Intelligence." Traditionally, many of us have referred to this inner power as "God" yet, ironically, it is the traditional, dogmatic view of God that oftentimes holds us back from our personal spiritual awakening. When we see God as external to us, it dims our inner light. When we see God as someone or something as all powerful, we allow ourselves to become powerless victims. When we see God as a rewarder or punisher, as a supernatural power we call on for help or to absolve ourselves from personal responsibility, we are unable to see ourselves as creators of the lives we are destined to live. It is my ardent hope that you will open your hearts and minds to the possibilities.

Many individuals, who call me and present a goal to achieve, are ultimately looking for bigger answers to life's questions. They are usually in a state of flux and somewhat disconnected from themselves and God. They may or may not go to a church. They are often not able to accept the literal interpretation of their religion's dogma and beliefs. As young children, even while being mesmerized by the metaphorical truth of the stories they were being told, they might question whether any of them could really be true. They long for a way to genuinely believe in a loving, kind God, but they feel helpless and hopeless about ever experiencing or finding this kind of God. They want a spiritual life, but they don't know where to begin. They are willing to discipline themselves if needed, but they want their efforts to be meaningful and relate to their everyday lives. Where is God for people like this?

This concept is for people who are unable to find a connection to an external God who limits and scares them—or even to an external God who loves them. It is for people who have almost given up their quest for a spiritual connection until they point their search inside. God doesn't step out of the clouds for these people; instead, they come to God through themselves. They come to realize that they are manifestations of God, and they must learn to recognize and develop the divine within themselves. When they do, the sky is the limit regarding their ability to create and manifest the life they seek.

A Process to Uncover your Divine Intelligence

Empowerment requires a game plan. People are eager to change but don't know how; I was once one of those people. I had never developed an inner spiritual guide, nor was I sourced from within. I had not yet discovered my true self, my own power, my own voice. To that end, I started having daily, honest conversations with my 'self' to reconnect with my inner voice and inner light. I eventually brought my thoughts, words and actions into alignment with my personal truths, values, and character.

And so can you. Everything begins with you. It all comes down to your relationship with your 'self.' You must commit to developing this relationship and make a conscious decision to awaken your Divine Intelligence. I will show you how.

The game plan that I created was a set of instructions and exercises to guide people to their inner light so they could then be guided by this inner light. I created a continuing conversation with one's highest self. *The Dialogues*, as they were known then, emerged in the early 1990s when I worked as a doctor in a major mental health facility in the field of counseling psychology. This environment became my laboratory for developing a process to make each of us the absolute authority in our own life and consciousness.

Psychologists call that having an *internal locus of control*. As I continue to evolve consciously, it has become the focus and intention of my life. **Locus of control** is the frame of reference for the extent to which individuals believe they can control their reactions to events that affect them. Generally speaking, a person with an external locus of control believes that fate or God controls his or her life; whereas a person with an internal locus of control believes that life is what we make of it.

I had earlier made this concept the focus of my dissertation study in graduate school. I now realize that the choices and events in my life were always pointing me toward the future discovery of a process to help people find and activate this creative power within them. I can now see that there was always a Divine Intelligence within me trying desperately to get my attention.

Over the past 35 years I have guided and empowered people who were looking for help with perplexing questions, solutions to personal crises, a path to achieve a goal, or simply, looking for "more" in their lives. Thousands of people have used my process to remove limiting beliefs and blocked emotions to get what they truly want. At the end of their self-discovery journeys, they found not only themselves but also a new sense of creative energy and an expanded view of God. Because of this revelation, a Dialogue has become a gateway to accessing and activating the Creator; thus, I began to refer to each movement forward toward our Divine Intelligence as the Divine Intelligence Process™ (or the "DI Process," for short).

Our Next Evolutionary Step

For thousands of years, we have not known or been able to accept the truth: God is also found inside all people—every one of us! Our next evolutionary step is to harness the power of our spiritual minds. Our powerful potential, our Divine Intelligence, is lying dormant in each of us.

I understand that when I present God as intelligence within, rather than or in addition to a being in the heavens, this idea will be met with controversy. But ideas that run counter to established beliefs are often met with resistance or dismissed as heretical. Examples abound. Copernicus and Galileo once dared to suggest that the Earth was not the center of the Universe, a departure from a long-held world view. Aristotle (et al.) posited the Earth was round while ancients insisted it was hollow or square, which is the implication set forth in the Bible. Suffice it to say that pioneers in any field expect such controversy and are undeterred in the face of scientific evidence to the contrary. Seeing is believing.

New scientific research is both supporting and supplanting long-held beliefs. You no longer have to wrestle with opposing world views. Simply expand your own. What Divine Intelligence teaches us is: What we say and do matters—not just to us personally, but to our collective consciousness. We are all a work in progress.

Uncover and embrace the mystery, the power, the goodness, and the divinity we all have within. Join me in reclaiming the divine within you. As this message spreads through the world and gains enough momentum, we can all, together, hasten the evolutionary pace of the human race.

Let's dare to evolve to our highest state. Let's decide to see God in everyone on this earth, including ourselves, and find heaven here on Earth. Let's all awaken the divine Creator within!

Dr. Jayne Gardner is the author of "*Divine Intelligence: A Scientific Process to Awaken the Creator Within*". The Second Edition is now available on Amazon.com and everywhere books are sold.

As a Thought Leader with a distinct philosophy of self-help, ethical living and mind-power metaphysics, Dr. Jayne Gardner believes that thought can radically transform circumstances. When people move their minds, they move their world. The Divine Intelligence Process became successful only because she first tested it out in her own life and then in the lives of hundreds of clients.

Dr. Gardner has presented seminars and workshops all over the United States and has represented many prestigious groups, such as the International Coach Federation, Centers for Spiritual Living, Unity Churches, and the Young Presidents Organization. She has presented her system for personal coaching on CNN's *Business Unusual*, as well as made several appearances on the *Good Morning Texas* show in response to current events.

She graduated with a Ph.D. from the University of North Texas in counseling psychology and is also a graduate of the Executive Coaching program at the University of Texas at Dallas (UTD). She is certified by the International Coach Federation as a Master Certified Coach (MCC), a designation awarded to fewer than 400 coaches worldwide. She has been on the faculty at Texas Christian University (TCU) and UTD and has coached Executive Master of Business Administration (EMBA) students at UTD. She owns her own coach training company called The Divine Intelligence Institute.

Continued…

Dr. Jayne Gardner
469-519-2727
drjayne@DivineIntelligenceInstitute.com
www.DivineIntelligenceInstitute.com

https://twitter.com/drjaynegardner
www.facebook.com/drjaynegardner
https://plus.google.com/+JayneGardner
www.youtube.com/channel/UCsoBhvgvl5XSrnz7DZGa98A
www.linkedin.com/in/jaynegardner/
www.instagram.com/drjaynegardner/

The Divine Intelligence Institute
1333 W. McDermott, Suite 150
Allen, Texas 75013

MELISSA NICKELSON

Live YOUR Life

What is your definition of living a fully productive life? Do you feel like you are making a difference? That is a question I have pondered most of my life. It is a difficult question that has different meaning for anyone you ask. One person's idea of fully living is different from someone else's. What has meaning to you? How do you live a full life? What engages you to live YOUR life?

At one point in my life, I felt as if my life was spinning out of control. My marriage was ending in divorce, my son was a toddler and I was trying to find a new career path. It was a tough time, and I felt like I was barely keeping my head above water. I knew this was not how I wanted to live, and I set out to change my life. It was not an easy decision or a fast one, but a necessary change. It took time and continued dedication to feel as if I was truly living an innergized life. While working in the area of family law, I saw that although the case was over, the pain and emotions remained. I felt compelled to help others realize that you have to learn to work through the emotional side; learning to trust yourself by feeling confident and moving into the next phase of live. I became a life coach intent on helping people find out who they are, what they want and how to get there. The more people I coached, the more I realized that my purpose in life is to work with others to find themselves and their confidence, just like I had to. I use myself as an example to others that you can change, you have to want to change and that it takes time and effort. I published a book I had floating around in my head for five years. It had been a goal of mine for a long time. It took time to get it out of my head and onto paper, but I never gave up. I kept working on it until it was finished. Never give up your dreams. Sometimes it takes longer to accomplish your dreams than you anticipate. Never give up. The end results are worth all of the work you put into them.

Working as a life coach and divorce coach has taught me a lot about myself. There are trying times, and times of pure joy. At the end of the day, if I have helped just one person feel alive again, I am happy. If my clients start to question their life in a good way and are ready to make changes, I have done my job. Dealing with clients at one of the worst times of their lives, and working with them on starting the next phase of their life, has purpose for me.

When people ask me what I do, I often get asked questions on how I help people. Once I explain what a life coach does, I frequently hear stories about how their daughter, their friend, or someone they know should call me. I spend a lot of time hearing stories from people who have issues or problems or the problems their friend has. Most people just want someone to listen, to really hear what they are saying. That is what I do.

Working with people who are ready to change, and will put in the time and effort it takes to make changes, is very rewarding. To watch someone who was an emotional mess move into a confident person, and make major changes in their life, is simply amazing.

Part of living your life, is finding out what you want to do, what you are passionate about. It is not always easy, and can cause waves with your friends and family. People mean well, but sometimes are not willing to take a risk, therefore they do not want you to take one either. Feeling safe and secure often times battles with having the confidence to step outside your comfort zone to make a change. If you feel as if you are battling other people's expectations of what you should be doing, it can hinder you and your outcome. This is where it is important to have the confidence to walk in your own shoes, not what someone else wants for you. To live YOUR life, not live someone else's life.

When I work with clients, and they start to truly live their life, I know I am doing what I set out to do, help people discover who they are and to live their life. Once you help someone find their confidence, and they move forward in life, they want others to feel good about themselves. Clients are the best source of referral, and it's rewarding to hear someone tell you a client talked about how you helped them. These are the days I strive for, to know that I made a difference. I have taken steps to live my life and know that what I do has meaning. I want to know that at the end of my life, I made a difference, if only to a few people. You affect the world one person at a time, and I try to accomplish this with my clients.

Just like working with clients to improve their life and feel more confident, I must continuously work on myself. I have to walk the path I encourage others to walk. I face difficult times and days, just like everyone else. I know I have a choice: I can see the hard, the difficult or, I can see the good. I try to focus on the good times, and work through the hard times. It is like seeing that one ray of sunshine on a cloudy day. I have to remember there will always be problems, yet I can choose to work through them or let them run my life. I do not want my life to be run by hurt, problems or drama. I want to live my life with a positive attitude, have confidence and believe I can and will face whatever life gives me. This is a life lesson I had to learn the hard way. If I can help shorten the learning curve for anyone, I have accomplished what I set out to do. I have fulfilled my passion and purpose.

It is important to me to live life, not just survive. We have all hit survival mode at some point in life, yet we should not live in survival mode. To live life, you must let go of things you cannot control, and focus on what you can. You must take things as they come, and not let the small problems become big problems. Living life means taking responsibility for yourself and your actions, and changing what needs to change, so you can enjoy life. When you are fully participating in your life, you feel alive. There will always be bumps in the road, but part of living life is how you handle the bumps. Do you keep moving, or are you stuck and cannot move past the bumps? Living fully engaged and INNERgized is to learn to handle life's speed bumps. Everyone lives at a different speed; your personal speed limit is the speed at which you move, and feel comfortable handling issues and life.

Having your own business is challenging and rewarding at the same time. I have learned to handle situations I never imagined. My motto is Choose Happy! Happiness is a choice. There are days I feel so happy, and there are days I struggle. Yet, at the end of the day, I choose to be happy. I once heard someone say the meaning of HOPE is to help one person every day. That one person may be you.

It is difficult to always help others if you are not helping yourself. There are times you must help yourself, so that you can continue to live your life.

Life is what you make it to be, are you living YOUR life?

Melissa Nickelson is a CDC Certified Divorce Coach® and Certified Mindset for Success Coach who works with clients in her private office in Fort Worth or via telephone. As a personal life coach, she specializes in working with those who are facing or considering life-changing choices. Her clients include those who are encountering everything from the process and fallout of divorce to career change to figuring out what's next. Melissa focuses on helping clients "choose happy"… which often means determining what makes them happy and then what steps are needed to get there. "Life may make choices for us, but we're never truly stuck; we always have options," she says.

Melissa is the author of *From Mrs. to Ms.: A Guide to Living Your Life During and After Divorce, The Family Law Attorney's Guide To Understanding and Dealing With Client's Emotions,* and *Thoughts Quotes and More Journal.*

Melissa lives in Fort Worth, Texas with her husband, Gary, a family law attorney, and two slightly spoiled dogs. Melissa was a family law legal assistant for seventeen years before becoming a life coach and certified divorce coach. She has been divorced and knows firsthand the emotional roller coaster that follows. Melissa works with clients individually and in group sessions to help work through the pain associated with the emotional side of divorce.

Her motto in life is: Choose Happy! Happiness is a choice.

Continued…

Melissa Nickelson
817-732-5267
office@MelissaNickelson.com
www.MelissaNickelson.com

www.linkedin.com/in/melissanickelson
www.instagram.com/melissanickelson
https://www.facebook.com/MelissaNickelsonLifeCoach
https://twitter.com/nickelsonm
https://pinterest.com/nickelson

5201 West Freeway, Suite 104
Fort Worth, TX 76107

MARILYN EAGEN

Follow Your Heart, Your Divine Inside

"What was the best advice you have ever received?" was proposed on a fun girls day out. As we took turns answering, I had to really think about the advice I have received from brilliant colleagues, teachers and friends. In a matter of seconds there were a plethora of clever and profound quotes running through my head. Not only insight I have received, but advice I have shared. Then I realized. It all came down to one answer. The one thing that I emphasize to my students, clients and friends: "Follow your heart, Your Divine inside." No matter how much wisdom, love and brilliance comes through your friends and others you trust, you still process it into what is truly best for you based on your own Divine inner wisdom.

This is especially important right now as our world is going through tremendous change. We are all faced with big and small decisions to make constantly. Finding a way to make these decisions easily is a beautiful gift to give yourself and those around you. Tapping into your own inner wisdom and listening to the answer whether it comes in a sensation, words, a sense of knowing or a sense of relief in your body can give you your answer. Using this on a daily basis gives you a sense of power in your life. You can become the Master of your own life instead of a victim of circumstances.

This doesn't mean that everything feels good and easy all the time. It means you have awareness of every situation while making appropriate choices for yourself with the intention of your highest good and the highest good of all.

The Peace Place a house I converted into a small energy community center and business space was threatened with flooding. The acre that it sits on and the acreage connected to this property are sacred and beautiful, sitting between two creeks. This would normally not be an issue; however, the greater suburban area has built levees to "control" the water from two large rivers around our city which changed everything. The past no longer can predict the future, which is truly the case for all the changes we are witnessing right now.

I was getting a lot of valuable advice on how to handle the situation, however, I couldn't do all of it in the time that was allowed. The human piece of me was saying to move a few valuables out, get things as high as possible, take precautionary measures with the electricity. The spiritual part of me knew what to do and many were advising me to not go overboard with physical work. My beautiful neighbor and I said many prayers and sent healing Reiki energy to the situation.

Yet, first I had to take a moment to breathe, see the beauty of nature and get quiet inside, connect to the Divine in my head and in my heart. As I thought about my situation, my body just wouldn't let me go through a lot of physical labor that felt unnecessary. My daughter and I decided to go outside and stand in the energy. I then got the message to do "my part". A Shamanic ceremony honoring all the elements of nature, the Divine that lived in nature and the ancestors and ancient energies that felt so present in that moment, seems to be what needed to be done as "my part". We continued to just BE in the beauty of this sacred space sending gratitude to all. We then noticed a bright golden cloud of light right above the property that felt so comforting to us. We knew that all was well.

Hopefully, we don't deal with things as heavy as flooding threats on a daily basis, however, everyday life brings little situations that can be supported by connecting into our hearts and our own inner-wisdom when they pop up.

At our invitation our daughter and her children moved in with us a few months ago. I chose to assist by offering to get the children ready and out the door in the mornings. This was a big adjustment for me as I have had total freedom in the mornings for several years. One morning, I had an early commitment, earlier than I would normally schedule. That morning seemed especially hectic with last minute problems showing up. The bus was late, the dog still needed to go out and we forgot to pack a water bottle for the preschooler. Unexpected little things put a little "edginess" in the morning.

My self-judgment kicked in full blast, "I teach self-care, energy exercises to manage these situations and well as many different approaches, I shouldn't feel this anxious over such silly little issues…" However, those feelings were present and I had a choice to beat up on myself or let that go and find a solution that felt good to all of us. So, I took a breath, looked at those children as the magical little creatures they are, and suddenly a new process I have been using popped into my head. I started using a mantra that helps shift energy. I asked my granddaughter to repeat these phrases as a fun game. "I am love, I am joy, I am peace, I am freedom, I am tranquility, I am wonder, I am bliss, I am beauty". She loved it and asked to do it again. It shifted energy for both of us and we then chose to have fun and enjoy our day. She happily went to her new preschool. And though it looked as if I would be late, I arrived to my meeting in plenty of time and a much better mood than it seemed it might be.

Most people experience situations similar to this on a daily basis. Big and small issues demonstrate how my perspectives in life changed. And of course, I have made many choices that may not have resulted in the easiest path. However, all were of great importance as far as learning how I want to feel in this life. We can tap into our own wisdom within and our own power of Being. We can, in time be our own master. I am not telling you exactly how that looks for you, because everyone will do it differently. That is the beauty in life, and we all have the opportunity to live in multidimensionality.

You may be wondering what I mean by that. Multidimensionality is the ability to see these issues in that higher perspective and live in connection with Divine wisdom and still appreciate our connection to the earth. I believe that as we continue to experience these massive changes on earth we are all here to help make these changes better for all of humanity. We all have a purpose on the earth. And working in the earthly purpose is much easier and effective if we can also be connected to our own personal Divine inside to support us. I will offer to you that having a daily practice of connection that works in your life is beneficial in moving into the space of trusting your inner guidance.

This is what becoming a Master of your own life is about. Choosing how you want to feel in every situation and knowing that there will be both easier and challenging times. Being present to the situation and intending the highest good of all while consulting your inner wisdom can bring light and laughter to the issue. An energy community is hugely important right now as changes and shifts move us into a new way of being. These shifts and changes are continuing to reveal the truth all around us, your intuition will continue to grow and blossom as you choose how you want to BE in the world. We are all in this together and we can choose to make it feel as easy as possible with love, laughter and community. Keep learning, connecting with the Divine and each other, and communicating with love and compassion. Then act based on your head and heart working together with Divine unconditional love at its center. If we all live in multidimensionality, we can navigate these changes in our world together with peace and ease.

Marilyn Eagen assists people in navigating change and challenges with ease and peace. Her business, **Harmony Healthcare**, uses an individualized and integrative approach in a gentle and spiritual way to assist you in moving forward on your journey. Marilyn is a Shaman, Certified Energy Medicine Practitioner, Women's Energy Coach, Certified Life Coach, and a Reiki Master Teacher in Usui, Karuna, Holy Fire and Celestial Reiki. She is also trained in many other modalities and utilizes them whenever it is appropriate. Marilyn is available to teach classes, speak at your gathering, and for Shamanic clearings, journeys and ceremonies. She is also schedules private, one-on-one sessions (in-office or via phone).

Marilyn also owns **The Peace Place**, a community cottage, available for energy gatherings, classes and workshops. Her Individual Journey program at The Peace Place gives you access to walk the labyrinth, use the Bio-mat, meditate, and other personal-growth activities, supporting you on your journey.

Marilyn also created a DVD, available via download on her website, full of "do-along" energy exercises, assisting you in your own daily practice. You can view a sampling of the DVD here: http://www.marilyneagen.com/the4essentialsvi.html

Continued...

Marilyn Eagen
314-330-4156
me@MarilynEagen.com
www.MarilynEagen.com

Facebook business page: https://www.facebook.com/holisticharmonylifecare/
Facebook Group Page: https://www.facebook.com/groups/940587469420527/
www.instagram.com/marilyneagen/
www.linkedin.com/in/marilyn-eagen-pta-eem-cp-195a701a/

2841 Barrett Station Rd.
Ballwin, MO 63021

GAIL GATES

Agingschmaging

How I came back to my creative fire in midlife, and why I want to help other women do the same.

"It's not just about creativity, it is about the person you're becoming while you're creating."

–Charlie Peacock

Do you remember your first time? No, not that first time! I mean the time you were about to pay for your groceries and the bagger said, "Would you like paper or plastic, Ma'am?" I do, and I was a little shocked. I looked around to see if there was a woman standing nearby who deserved the title. Was someone's pearl necklaced grandmother or sensible-shoe wearing great aunt behind me? Nope. The high school kid was looking straight at me. "Ma'am?"

That's the thing with aging and feminine identity. How others view us, define us, or talk to us influences our perceptions and self-esteem. Don't even get me started on how the media and marketing guru's depict women! As women we become increasingly aware that growing older comes with baggage we didn't pack but have to carry. Toss in the menopausal transition and it's easy to get lost. Or, found, in my case. Perhaps my story may sound familiar.

"In the end, all you are is a story. Make it a good one."

–From the movie *Australia*

I was a single mom of two teenagers as my 40th birthday crept closer. It was sobering to think that in a very short time my children would leave home to start adult lives. 40 years old. When did that happen? Was life potentially half over? My work as a dental assistant was enjoyable, but there was a restlessness I found hard to ignore. Was I where I thought I'd be at this point in my life? NO! How many goals had I set and actually met?

My daily work commutes found me daydreaming about "someday." I imagined quitting my job, buying art supplies, and moving to a tiny cabin near a rural lake. Being close to water always calmed and stirred me at the same time. If I did that, how could I sustain myself financially going forward? What did I need? What brought me joy, and what, in my heart of hearts, did I want?

Almost as though a ray of light filtered through my thought-fog, it happened. I.Was. Thinking. About. Myself.

That's against the law for women, isn't it? We are socially conditioned from birth to put the needs of others first, and shamed for putting our desires into words and actions. What was going on?

Everything seemed foreign and familiar, wrong and right, scary and possible. I was changing, but I had no idea how to control any of it. Who could I talk to about midlife crazy? What role models were out there to follow...or that I wanted to follow?

My friends were in a different "aging" place. Most didn't want to talk about midlife, menopause, or growing older. "We're fine, you're fine," they insisted. "Let it go." But, I couldn't. I'm an information seeker, so I began reading books by Dr. Christiane Northrup, Dr. Tieraona Low Dog, and Susun S. Weed. Through them I came to realize what I was experiencing was positive and empowering.

The unexpected gift? When my focus changed from fear to a newfound sense of control, my life changed. For the better!

Was it hard? Sometimes. I tend to be a pleaser. Shedding the behaviors and people who were not supporting my ongoing transition took strength. Old habits and happiness-sucking people did not go away without some nasty moments. But the more I understood and cleared the negatives from my life, the more I attracted goodness. New people emerged. Wonderful, "how-can-we-help-you," women held their hands out to me. A handsome, kind, man asked if I would consider letting him "court" me. How charming is that in this day and age? Opportunities I had never considered appeared, as did the courage to act. It felt dangerous to put myself first...surely lightning would strike me down...but it also felt decadent and delicious. I didn't know what I was doing, but I was letting it happen.

The courtship turned into a blissful marriage. My children ventured off to find their way in the big world, so I decided it was time for me to do the same. There were many interests I had been putting off. The question, "If not now, when?" became my mantra. I quit my job and returned to college.

> "Live as if you were to die tomorrow. Learn as if you were to live forever."
> –Mahatma Gandi

The first degree was in Integrative Health and Healing to deepen my understanding of our human wholeness. I segued that education into a Bachelor's degree focused on women's issues. Still hungry, I earned a Masters of Liberal Studies degree, which fed my artistic fires. Writing, photography, and silk scarf dying gave me a way to express my new identity and feelings. The more I grew into my role as artist and "aging" woman, the more gratitude I felt. My happiness was a blessing that needed sharing. I wondered how I could help other women who were also feeling lost in midlife. There needed to be a way of connecting, creating safe places to ask intimate questions, and to give and receive support.

I decided to offer "Playshops" where women gather, share stories on transitioning or whatever is on their minds and then paint silk scarves to keep. The creative beauty that women explore and welcome at these events is magical, healing, and unifying.

My blog, agingschmaging.com, is mostly musings that concern female aging. Sometimes funny, sometimes cathartic, the writing is a portal. The goal is to encourage women to tell their stories because they have read mine. We all go through highs, lows, and periods of "what the !@#$ just happened?" I believe our accumulated experiences uplift us all if we are willing to reveal them. I love the work, and I love talking with women.

However.

I am an introvert. My creative fire and general wellness is fanned by periods of solitude. Whereas I can give my undivided attention to others for stretches of time, the "aloneness" of photography restores me. For years I would take pictures of interesting and beautiful moments, and then hide them away in boxes and albums. Nobody else needed to see the photographs.

One day a friend said, "I know you take pictures. Why don't you enter one in the local fair? It's fun, and no big deal." What a terrifying idea. Not only would my photo be judged officially, but judged by friends, neighbors, and complete strangers. I stewed about it for weeks. In the end, believing no risk equals no growth, I entered. A few days later my friend phoned to say I won the Grand Reserve ribbon in the photography division.

It's funny how a little pebble creates a big ripple. Getting the ribbon bolstered my confidence. I then applied for, and received, an individual artist grant. The requirements included finding a mentor, but whom? My prayers were answered. The stars aligned and led me to Dee Kotaska. Our first meeting felt as though we had known each other for a lifetime. Dee taught me about the emotional connection inherent in excellent images, and of the creative power of iPhone apps. Traditional photography is the cornerstone, but now I have the tools to turn my photos into impressionistic art that excites me.

Because of the opportunities the grant provided, I have met accomplished photographers I would never, ever, have had the courage to approach earlier. For instance, Dee and I traveled to Lake Tahoe to take an "iPhoneographer" class with two top talents, Lynette Sheppard, and Teri Lou Dantzler. Surrounded by that much creative energy was a catalyst to reach even further.

In the past year I have been a featured artist, given a solo photographic gallery, and have shared a gallery with Dee. If you had told the younger me that taking a tiny risk such as entering a photo in the county fair would have altered my artistic world, I would not have believed it possible.

My dream is to continue writing to and for women, and to keep honing my photographic skills and creativity. Agingschmaging is my website and is mostly a springboard for my blog.

My creative resurgence is intended to inspire yours too! Please check out my photography at https://gailgates.smugmug.com I will slowly be adding galleries to my site.

Many years ago a high school kid called me "ma'am," and it made me feel old. No, I let it make me feel old, when I had no idea what being old meant. I still don't know. Menopause brought the end of my childbearing years, but unending new beginnings.

It is my sincere hope this transition will be the same for you. Ask yourself what you do that makes you lose track of time because it is so much fun. How can you do more of that? Is it possible to live our dreams in the second half of life?

Yes, Ma'am. It is.

Gail Gates: Agingschmaging

Gail Gates is the storyteller and award-winning photographer of Agingschmaging.com, a place dedicated to the wonders of aging as women. Returning to college in midlife, scared sh**less, she realized there were many women also questioning their new "second-half" identities, voices, and creative fires. After obtaining her Masters of Liberal Studies, she began profiling women through stories and photographs. Her focus is on women who have the courage to find their happiness regardless of cultural norms and pressures.

She lives in Minnesota with her "please-don't-write-about-me-again husband," Tad, a plant destroying Siberian Husky, Booker, and two rescue cats, Pudgy and Giese, who remain stubbornly oblivious that they needed rescuing.

Gail Gates
888-608-3166
gatega1958@msn.com
www.AgingSchmaging.com

www.facebook.com/agingschmaging?ref=hl
www.pinterest.com/gatega1958/
https://twitter.com/gatega1958?lang=en

SHANNON SCHINDLER REDMAN

Empowering YOU to Know Your Own Greatness

Less than 5 years ago, it occurred to me, I was broken in every area of my life. I was well over 200 pounds, had spent 18 years in corporate tax and accounting, was stuck working in a cube and I had 3 jobs. I was earning what most would say was good money. Yet was $39,474.71 in credit card debt and barely surviving. I was in a 13-year marriage that was not working. And more importantly I wasn't able to be the MOM I wanted to be.

An A'HA moment in time led me to a new view of my own life. I discovered I was just trying to survive and get through my own life. I asked myself, **"How long was I willing to keep pretending everything was ok…while putting up with my current set of circumstances?"** Confronting this thought made me mad. And then I was hooked—hungry—and I set out to be the best version of me I could be.

At the time I couldn't see it, but I knew I had to set an example for my daughter. I knew I had to break the generational chains of poverty, poverty-mentality and the way my life was heading. I was a 3rd generation accountant and it is clear today that I was not meant for that grey cube with florescent lights flickering overhead. I was working in a rigid environment, where "if it wasn't a number that went on a tax return, I was not allowed to speak it." Although different, I was living my life at home much the same way.

I began seeking out teachers who had traveled a similar path and who had discovered their own hidden greatness. They had a vision and the method that uncovered a seed in me. Surprisingly, this greatness—this heart—had been there all the time. I had just not been present to it. Now producing fruits far beyond what my own imagination could ever have dreamed back then.

Consider YOU having your own seed, living in you, waiting to be distinguished and then nurtured. This discovery was challenging to receive at first, and something inside of me knew to say, "YES!" I am wondering if there isn't something inside of you, wanting… needing… to be unleashed? Consider it so!! I welcome you! I probably "get" how you feel. I have felt that same way too.

In 2012, my reinvention began… from the ground up and from nothing. The first project was The Fun Flirty and Fabulous 5 & 5, a 5k/5mile run in St. Louis. A passion project which took less than 90 days to mobilize, using the power of social media and systems. We had over 600 runners, and amazing sponsors with Whole Foods, Sports Authority and Michelob Ultra. Featured on several radio shows and online shows, we created a community of women in a movement revolution. It wasn't just about the race or finishing the project—it was really about challenging and uniting women in something bigger than they knew themselves to be, and they responded. The passion, dreams and vision turned into a success and I could see what else might BE POSSIBLE. I recognized my talents in marketing and sales and knew I COULD create something different. I began surrounding myself with people who listened for my greatness, created an environment where I accessed success and raised my consciousness.

I'm wondering what greatness is asleep within you?

In October 2013, I brought Wise Women Connect to St. Louis, started it from scratch, and grew it for a year as an empowering women's networking organization. We impacted over 300 women-owned businesses, offering access to expertise for branding both themselves and their business, with target marketing and social media. We created and offered training in strategic business-building and mindset activities, helping them to differentiate themselves in the marketplace. In less than a year, we had many success stories; two of my favorites are a financial planner achieving 1 million in sales and an Insurance broker tripling her business. Both contribute their success to this vulnerable and safe space we created while meeting for lunch twice a month.

This was in me all along. It was a matter of becoming conscious of my value and power within. Inside this reinvention journey of mine, I have had the pleasure and honor to create projects and give back with community impact. With the money raised from the Fun Flirty and Fabulous 5&5 event, we made a profound difference in the lives of our participants LOCALLY, and were able to drill a desperately-needed fresh water well in Kenya, Africa, impacting families, a local primary school with 314 students, a church, and a community center there and it continues today. We have also donated thousands of dollars to Bridgeway Women's Center for the expansion of their facilities, where they are committed to providing a safe-haven for women and their children, as they escape their violent partner. One woman in four will experience domestic violence—this is something I am very passionate about supporting. We also have been able to contribute monthly for the last 5 years to a local spiritually-based radio station, Joy FM supported by its listeners. They provide Music, Faith and Community.

More recently, we have begun monthly sponsorships of children though VivaKids.org. A VivaKids sponsorship provides a child with things such as a quality education, nutritious diet, healthcare when needed, spiritual and personal mentoring, and vocational and life-skills training. The best part was when our family went on a mission trip to meet them.

Continuing to expand my reinvention, I had built a professional career by March 2016, and it was official—I was a million-dollar sales woman and #1 in the company. I went from a cube job to a sales job in construction and BEGAN to CREATE my life with no degree, no experience, no networking events. By the end of 2016, I hit 2-million in sales, working part time for the construction company. How does that happen? I developed systems for my business to work smarter, not harder. It became one of my favorite things to teach! I took the rest of the year to travel the world, share the POWER of SYSTEMS that work and promote the idea that your work and play are almost the same. I say yes to having it all!

By now I had built MULTIPLE MILLION DOLLAR businesses FOR OTHERS and thought why not for me?!?! January 13th, 2017, I jumped into opening my own business as a Direct Sales Rep with Kangen Water...much like building an airplane in midair after it's already left the ground...LMAO. 100% working for myself from anywhere in the world. Within 150 days, I was able to quit my construction J.O.B., and in 208 days achieved the TOP income level. Many people said I wouldn't succeed and some even laughed. The difference between them and me? I'm living from a vision for my life. Committed to empowering myself to find and develop my greatness. Now, I'm committed to assisting other women find theirs.

Are you interested in identifying your passions and expanding your life?

The RISE of Woman coaching platform was born from these experiences. I now coach passionate sales-women, entrepreneurs, and network marketing professionals who are ready to live the abundant and purpose-driven lifestyle they've previously only dreamt of. Today, I teach business building, brand identity, online marketing and magnetic influence and mindset in the "The RISE of Woman" signature program.

Clients receive the confidence and community they need to be powerful, visible, and unstoppable business owners, entrepreneurs and home-based business woman-preneurs! Learn more at www.TheRiseofWoman.com or schedule a complimentary private coaching session at www.WorkWithShannon.com

Humbled by my journey, yet thrilled that I discovered secrets to winning for women like me. People whose only real credentials are a willingness to work and a burning desire to "be somebody" (maybe more HEART than recognized talent). I want to share those secrets with you who are yearning to do something special with your life and not knowing where to begin. As I said earlier… I couldn't have imagined any of this. It all starts with you having the yearning and then the courage to take the next step—let's see what we can create!!

Shatter your limits and TRANSCEND YOUR FEARS! This is your time to step into your authentic power and discover your own greatness. **What would your life look like if you were "FREE" to create a business and life you love?**

Shannon Schindler Redman is an International Business Coach and founder of the premier business program, "The Rise of Woman". Shannon specializes in assisting passion-driven women to recognize bring their skills to the world and develop thriving businesses with international reach.

Shannon spent 18 years in corporate tax and accounting. She plunged into marketing and social media in October 2012. She successfully launched several community impact projects and a women's networking organization. April 2014 Shannon reinvented herself in sales, marketing and coaching businesses. Since then she has become a multi-million-dollar producer, working part time, raising a daughter, and traveling the world.

Today Shannon works with both new and experienced business women, entrepreneurs, and network marketing professionals through online business coaching and direct sales. "Despite the fact my clients didn't have any prior experience, they became rock stars in their own respective businesses, and producing their first million in sales with ease." Applying relatable real-life experiences to coaching, Shannon assists transform the lives of passionate women who desire to bring their skills and business to the world, make an impact, follow their purpose, and create free and abundant lives.

A speaker on several occasions for a variety of events including, the Unbelievable Women, Power Connection Network, Escape the 9 to 5 Grind Podcast, Richer Soul Podcasts and many more.

Continued…

Shannon Schindler Redman
314-494-7187
me@ShannonSchindlerRedman.com
www.ShannonSchindlerRedman.com
Online Coaching Program, www.TheRiseOfWoman.com
Schedule a complimentary private coaching session www.workwithShannon.com

www.facebook.com/shannon.schindler.redman
www.facebook.com/ShannonSchindlerRedmanTribe
www.linkedin.com/in/shannonschindlerredman/
https://twitter.com/sschindler14
www.instagram.com/shannonschindlerredman/

LISA HAUTLY

A Matter of Wellness

I arise in the morning torn between a desire to improve the world and a desire to enjoy the world. This makes it hard to plan the day.

E. B. White

I really want to save the world, but I also want to head to the lake. I want a healthier community, but I like breakfast dates and research tangents and clean laundry. All activities that bring me wellness at 58 years old, but delay my long-term vision of improving community wellbeing. Is it possible to have a successful wellness practice and a personally fulfilling life, echoing E. B. White's sentiments of improving the world while enjoying it? Shouldn't all wellness professionals? Actually, shouldn't all humans have an opportunity to develop a balanced life plan, one enjoyable moment at a time?

A year ago, I put on my favorite dress and with full intention, headed to the grocery store as a corrective step toward purposeful aging. I had finished coursework for my Health Education doctorate, and ironically, integrated some negative health behaviors (formerly known as bad habits:), such as lack of sleep, long sitting sessions, carry out foods, and high stress. Like a cardiologist who smokes, I wasn't quite practicing what I was preaching and it was time to make a change.

We sometimes forget that grocery shopping is a privilege, as is self-care when choosing healthy foods. I walked the aisles, and slowly, gratefully, filled my cart with the foods that support active aging and longevity. Fruits, vegetables, whole grains, seeds, nuts. And dark chocolate, because, researchers don't lie. It was the first literal step in a year long health quest supporting the belief we can improve our world and enjoy it at the same time. We may not have a comprehensive life plan, especially if we're lacking a clear vision, but we can use the past to refine our purpose. While the rest of my journey is unfolding, I'm excited to share lessons from the past, and the reason all of our journeys should matter.

Where I've Been

My journey is a bit predictable if you've spent any time reading midlife transition books, where passing through to the next life stage brings a new countenance that comes from discovering latent strengths. Books like Sarah Lightfoot's *The Third Chapter*, spotlight people who've hit their strides at midlife, with new career paths, volunteer positions, and passionate journeys. Every day we read stories of engineers turned teachers, hedge fund managers starting non-profits, retired artists creating knitting circles. I wanted a similar narrative.

I was hitting a midlife slump, where I noticed a widening gap between my actions and my passion. It wasn't a clichéd crisis, but I couldn't have defined my passion at that point. Where was that purpose-driven sense of connectivity and contribution to society, that I now know is a beautiful blend of emotional, social, and spiritual health? I was circling projects at work, and some days felt like I was morphing into a prototype of every marketing professional I'd met. After all, we got paid to create facades.

I became very aware of my energy levels when participating in wellness events. I loved sharing healthy recipes on local TV segments and at health expos. Perhaps it's the type of people who attended wellness events, or perhaps it was the result of healthy-minded people coming together to make change. In either case, I began fostering health promotion projects, where my marketing expertise felt mission-driven.

At the same time, I was growing concerned that the bulk of "health" information in the media was actually illness and treatment oriented. Advertorials posing as news, with cosmetic surgery ads targeting young women in the sidebars. Sure, pharmaceutical sponsored news can be useful, but few outlets seemed to be addressing wellbeing, where simple lifestyle changes had a profound impact. I called the editor of a local newspaper one day after reading more of the same, and asked "Do you ever cover wellness in your health section? Does health have to be associated with a product purchase?" I suggested he provide wellness-oriented resources that are low or no cost.

To which he replied, "Would you like to be a weekly columnist?"

It was time to launch my wellness business.

What I learned

Lesson One. I wasn't an expert. In fact, I was quite naive, like the office intern ready to tackle the world until the first dose of reality hits that this is a whole lot bigger than it appears. While I held Bachelor and Master degrees, I had absolutely no formal health science education, despite having read volumes of health data over many years. In other words, I was a well-read hobbyist, like a thousand others. I researched wellness programs, focusing on health coaching and personal training certifications. A small start, but the framework for my wellness business was birthed.

Lesson Two. We're fixated on skinny. Not surprisingly, my schedule filled quickly with midlife women. No other population is as open and honest as midlife women discussing their vision of wellness (and bra issues and senior moments and tender love stories). Yet, the gap between that vision and the longing to be skinny made program implementation challenging at best. I saw a willingness to risk long term health for a shot at thinness. I recognized it after years in food marketing, where "natural" and "healthy" claims are splattered across package labels. But now I was seeing it from the client side, where the health effects were evident. It's as if midlifers are programmed to worship an ideal that throttles the very root of wellbeing. We allow the entertainment/media industry to define acceptable body types. The patterns are similar across many other areas of our lives. Influencers tell us what to eat, how to think, what to wear, who to vote for, what to purchase. Of course we'd allow them to set our ideal weight. And naturally, that perceived ideal weight is closely tied to our sense of wellbeing, setting the stage for disordered eating, obsession with fitness as a metric of success, and high stress eroding our wellbeing. This is not healthy living and not the foundation for my wellness practice.

Lesson Three. Formal education matters. My cognitive behavioral coaching model was failing me. How do I promote whole health and the breadth of dimensions that contribute to overall wellbeing? Far greater than a dress size or a fitness feat, they are interrelated across physical, emotional, social, intellectual, and spiritual domains.

It was clear that psychological wellbeing and quality of life are elusive metrics when physical health is the singular focus. While it's logical that a healthy body is a foundational element of wellness, it isn't the *only* foundational component, or, arguably, even the most important. After basic needs are met, spiritual health or purposeful living becomes the framework on which all health dimensions are built. Stated another way, if the wheel of wellness includes components of the mind, body, and spirit, then an obsession with any single dimension brings unbalance and the wheel of life cannot roll efficiently.

I needed a more comprehensive approach. One that would address anxiety with physical and social solutions. One that would provide a framework where weight loss is a naturally occurring by-product of a whole health journey. Ultimately, I landed in a Health Education doctoral program, where health promotion is built on a holistic framework that prioritizes community-based health, while supporting personal wellbeing. It's a health professional team approach to improving the full spectrum of whole health.

Why it matters

You and I have far more in common than we're led to believe. We're just as interrelated and interdependent as our dimensions of health. Your health is my health. Your wellbeing is mine. Your community is mine. We're aging together and what we're experiencing collectively is increased depression and chronic illnesses in midlife women. Hardly the definition of purposeful aging.

I believe I can make a difference by sharing a message of whole health, where physical health meets emotional wellbeing. Where social health plays a supporting role in achieving physical goals and spirituality. I'm now empowered to develop evidence-based health promotion programs that educate and motivate women across a wide swath of communities. And if you believe in a ripple effect, you can see that your steps toward health-centered, purposeful aging can impact your family, friends, coworkers, community, and society at large. That's a powerful role for midlife women as we model wellbeing for future generations.

Maybe your first step isn't grocery shopping for longevity. Maybe it's joining a health minded book club or listening to a spiritual podcast daily. Maybe it's adding some breathing exercises into your workday to reduce your stress. Wherever you intentionally step into whole health, you'll not only reap the benefits personally, but you'll improve your community health. Like E. B. White, you'll have the option of improving the world and enjoying it along the way. And that matters to me.

Lisa Hautly: A Matter of Wellness

Lisa Hautly is a Certified Health Education Specialist (CHES), improving wellbeing in midlife and older populations through education, motivation, and the fostering of behavior changes. As a health promoter, author, speaker, and coach, Lisa develops whole health programs based on the following principles::
- Wellbeing occurs at the intersection of physical, mental, social, intellectual, and spiritual health.
- There's no mystery to healthy, purposeful aging; it is attainable by improving our environment and daily health habits.
- Wellness occurs on a continuum. Every choice is either making us more healthy or less healthy.

Lisa currently serves as chair of the St. Louis County Older Adult Commission, as a board member for Mental Health America of Eastern Missouri, and the Spirit of Women's Health Advisory Board. She received the 2015 Healthy Women Award from St. Luke's Hospital for her commitment to personal and community health. She holds a BA in Public Relations, an MA in Media Communications, and is currently working on her dissertation to complete her doctorate in Health Education.

Her ideal day includes family, sunshine, and a paddle board.

Continued…

Lisa Hautly
314-825-6557
lisa@LisaHautlyWellness.com
www.LisaHautlyWellness.com

www.linkedin.com/in/lisahautly/
www.facebook.com/lisa.hautly
www.facebook.com/lisahautlywellness/
www.instagram.com/lisahautly/
@lisahautly

THERESA JEEVANJEE, PhD

See What Love Can Do

Twenty-seven years ago, I was blessed with the sweetest boy. I only got to hold him a few minutes before he was whisked away for tests. He failed the APGAR, had a hole in his heart, the sutures around his soft spot were closed, and on and on the bad news came. Still in pain from the emergency C section, I kept hearing explanations such as "If the sutures are fused, when his head starts to grow, his brain will explode." Really, even if true, who says things like that to first-time mothers?

A few days later came the overall diagnosis, "The very rare Partial Trisomy 12 (there are only 12 in the medical literature and none exactly like his), which means mental and physical handicaps." Afterwards, the doctor shared his prediction, "If he makes it through the week, *which is unlikely*, he won't live past 4 years."

I am not a statistician, but even then I thought, "Who can make predictions on a sample set of 12, much less one." It did not matter, I was already in love, and that was the beginning of our journey.

Much later, I shared a version of this story with a young PT and she wisely said, "See what Love can do." Indeed. When he was 16, the square of his predicted life span (Did I mention my PhD is in math?), we had a "See What Love Can Do" party with over 100 people. As our journey continues, many people have loved and continue to love my dear Ryan to 27.

Most writers I know say that they do not have a choice in writing. It is as though a writer is "pregnant" with the book or story or poem. It has to come out. That is the way it was with *Dear Ryan*. I started writing *to* him before he was born. Then I wrote stories *about* him and his sisters. Those stories often included chronicles of our journey through "Western medicine," but often they were stories of dancing through life with all of its challenges. At some point, I thought that battles we won and triumphs we made might help others in similar situations. I felt a strong pull to share our journey with others.

Finding out that Ryan had an extremely rare chromosome disorder (his particular manifestation of partial trisomy 12 is unique) felt like the worst possible news. However, I soon realized it was the greatest blessing. Sharing that with parents in a similar situation might help them realize they are not alone. They might be comforted by some of our stories. They might use the book as a resource. They might feel inspired by our journey. They might even learn some helpful things about medicine, genetics, law, and people. We might connect so that we could learn from each other.

Dear Ryan is filled with lessons I have learned on this journey, most of them the "hard way." As a formerly very shy introvert, one of the first lessons I learned was that I needed to be an advocate for Ryan. I would need to speak up, to stand up, to question even the experts, and would often need to be relentless in these tasks. Much, much later I learned that in order to continue to advocate for Ryan, I would need to advocate for myself.

And that is exactly what has happened in the short time that the *Dear Ryan* has been published. I have met some amazing people and their tribes because of this journey. I have gotten feedback, including almost all five-star ratings with meaningful comments that the book has done exactly what I hoped: it has comforted, inspired, and educated those caring for a disabled child, those who love them, or those affected by them. That is essentially all of us.

"Innergized" is a term I love. It has energy at its core, but an energy that comes from within. One of my nicknames is The Energizer Bunny—I am pretty sure I have undiagnosed hyperactivity. I was born with a lot of energy and do not seem to require a lot of sleep. That is very good since there always seems to be a great deal of work and never enough sleep.

And I have been spiritual since I can remember. For me the idea that we are driven or have our energy from Inside is a beautiful way to say we are guided by the Holy Spirit, or however you name the Divine. Having a word for that: Innergized, is brilliant.

Even though I was often successful at "Letting go and letting God," I was not always successful in allowing the Holy Spirit to guide my *whole* day, rather than just the easy parts. So, I had to learn about Innergized Living, although I did not call it that.

Making rainbows out of rain is a key component to Innergized living. I had to figure out how to do this on many occasions. Even for the most simple of tasks.

Sometimes the Hardest Thing is a Haircut

Dear Ryan,

You were born with a thick head of wavy, dark hair. I love to run my fingers through it when you let me. You had your first hair cut at 4 months and have had them about every month since then. Except for a tough, rather long, period when you would not let anyone get near your face or head. I have memories of three of us holding you down while you hit and kicked just so we could get the hair out of your eyes.

Those years were tough, and not just because you would not let anyone cut your hair. It is interesting to me that I have put most of the difficulty of watching you go through so much pain out of my mind, and the one thing I remember is a special haircut. But, then again, it was not really the haircut that was the most special.

We had taken you to the auxiliary unit of St. Louis Children's Hospital. I do not remember the name of the unit nor do I know if it is even still there. At the time, it was next to the hospital and served children who had needs somewhere between the emergency room and the full hospital. We needed to call for an appointment, but it could be the same day. And you were usually out later the same day.

This time, the stay involved anesthesia. As you lay there deeply sleeping off the anesthesia, I thought, "Now would be a great time to give you a haircut." As I looked around the place, filled with white beds and sterile equipment, I realized there was probably no way they would let me. But, I asked one of the nurses anyway. I seem to recall his name was Mike. He was a very kind nurse, and listened with compassion as I explained how hard it was to give you a haircut. I even told him the story of the last attempt. He smiled with compassion, but said, "I am sorry, but I cannot give you permission to do that." I am sure my sigh was audible.

A few minutes later, he walked back in, smiled at you sleeping, and put a towel and a pair of scissors about a foot away from me. Before he left, he added, "No one else will be here for an hour. Let me know if you need anything else." I quietly cut your beautiful hair, and took a luxurious moment to run my fingers through it. I think you may have smiled in your sleep.

Mike must have been watching from somewhere because just as I finished and started to clean up, he came in and said, "I will do that." And he did. I could not thank him because that would acknowledge permission, but I hoped my smile said it all. And I thanked God for nurses like Mike who really seem to understand how sometimes the hardest thing in caring for a child is a haircut.

Love,
Mom

Grateful, I am.
Life is Good.

Theresa Jeevanjee

Theresa Jeevanjee, Ph.D teaches mathematics and computer science for MEGSSS (Mathematics Education for Gifted Secondary School Students) and computer science at Nerinx Hall High School. She enjoys running, painting, cooking, and taking ballet classes. She is an associate in the CSJ (Congregation of St. Joseph) community and is active in two prayer groups. Her volunteer work includes tutoring mathematics and helping with the theatre and chorus costumes for Nerinx Hall.

She and her husband live in Webster Groves, Missouri, with their adult children, Ryan, Kiran, and Lauren, and their two dogs, Ebony and Kuki.

To contact the author, please email faithandrelentlesslove@gmail.com.

For more information, please visit www.faithandrelentlesslove.com.

Theresa Jeevanjee
314-962-3392
FaithAndRelentlessLove@gmail.com
www.FaithAndRelentlessLove.com

www.facebook.com/tjeevanjee

CATHY SEXTON

Turning Bombshells Into Blessings

We all have a story. And we all face challenges in our professional and personal lives. But how many of us are grateful for those challenges and see the value they bring? Learning to be grateful for the bombshells in life is a challenge in itself. But I've learned those bombshells can be blessings that lead us to where and who we're meant to be—if we let them.

There was a time when my life was just humming along. I had my share of daily challenges, like everyone else, but I was married to the love of my life, had a beautiful daughter and step-daughter I loved dearly, and was surrounded by wonderful family and friends. Life was good. I was blissfully unaware of the twists and turns my life would take or the looming bombshells that would test and shape me.

You could say my first bombshell was self-inflicted. I had a good job in the corporate world, but I was a workaholic and was literally killing myself trying to keep up and even get ahead. I wanted to succeed. I wanted to be an excellent employee. I wanted to be known as that worker who came in early and stayed late to get the job done. But I also had a family I loved at home who needed my time and attention. I wanted to be everything to them and succeed in my personal life too. I wanted to do it all and have it all. There just weren't enough hours in the day.

My drive to do it all and have it all started taking its toll. I was stressed, overwhelmed, and exhausted. My doctor was telling me that my workaholic ways were causing catastrophic changes to my body and deep down I knew it was true. But I didn't know how to get off the hamster wheel. What could I possibly give up and still fulfill my definition of success in my life?

I did try to follow the doctor's recommendations, but I felt that backing off would be a failure in one area or another. It wasn't long before old habits returned and the bombshell dropped. It's said that 80 percent of health issues are caused by stress. In 2003, I became a statistic.

It was a wake-up call that gave me my first big lesson in the importance of work-life balance. Because I hadn't listened to or learned from those early warning signs, I was diagnosed with a stress-induced, life-threatening disease. I had pushed myself to the limit and came close to making my husband a widower and leaving my daughter without a mother. The thought of not being here anymore hit me hard. This was no longer just a warning, this was real, and I finally got it. Something needed to change. I had some decisions to make.

I started rethinking my choices in life. What did I really value? Which was more important, my work or my family? With what I was facing, the answers were clear. So, I left my job, struck out on my own, and opened a bookkeeping business. By doing this, I felt I could finally get a handle on my workaholic ways. I'd have the freedom to schedule my own time and work for my own prosperity, rather than the profits of an employer. Success could be measured on my own scale. I boldly embraced the chance to redesign my future. Again, life was good.

Business was good too—strong and steady. I had five employees, and had found a better work-life balance. In 2007, as the business continued to grow, I took on a partner. I found that sharing the responsibilities enabled me to have an even greater work-life balance and I was back to humming along—until the next bombshell dropped.

Two years after forming our partnership, my partner locked me out of my own business. I was devastated. I felt betrayed and confused. I had to file bankruptcy, because the business and all the debt were in my name. Everything I had achieved and worked so hard for crumbled around me, and I had no idea where to go from there. It was one of the most horrible experiences of my professional life. One I wasn't sure I could ever recover from.

As horrible as that situation was, it once again caused me to do some serious soul searching. In the days and weeks after, I spent time cursing fate, wondering why this was happening to me, and throwing myself the occasional pity party as I worked through my grief and disbelief. But an interesting thing happened as the weeks passed and I dug deep to figure out what came next. As the anger and frustration faded, my eyes were opened to a path I had never even considered and I started to see the blessings in that bombshell.

I realized everything that had happened over the past nine years could have a greater purpose. It was all an opportunity to redirect my career to one that was a much better fit for me. I had learned so much about myself, life, running a business, and how important it is to create our lives based on our values, so we create a life we value. I had a passion for helping others align their lives in a way that allowed them to experience success both personally and professionally, without the stress. And it all fit perfectly with my strengths as a person. From those years of struggle came revelation, and *The Productivity Experts* was born.

Once the light bulb went on, I started to see a path ahead of me. It turned into an exciting time full of growth and possibilities. I set out to learn everything I could to help others avoid the pitfalls and minefields I had unintentionally, but successfully, navigated. I immersed myself in study on mindset, organization, effective coaching, and innovative solutions to the financial aspects of growing a successful business. I uncovered strengths I wasn't even aware I had and began thinking about how those strengths would fit with my new path and benefit my clients.

In the years after *The Productivity Experts* was founded, bombshells continued to fall, though they have come from events in my personal life. They included serious medical issues for family members and friends, as well as losses of people I loved dearly. Every year was marked with one or more of these life challenges. But again, each instance brought opportunities for digging deeper and learning more about myself and what truly mattered in my life. I also gained greater insight into the challenges of running a business when the hard things in life are happening all around you.

Alex Elle is quoted as saying, "I'm thankful for my struggle because without it I wouldn't have stumbled across my strength." In my case, my passion for helping clients take their businesses to the next level and achieve their business goals might have gone undiscovered without the struggles I faced personally and professionally. It's not about what happens to us as our stories unfold, it's about how we choose to respond to the bombshells we face. I've learned to be grateful for all of it—the good, the bad, and the ugly. I don't think of my glass as half empty or half full. I'm just grateful I have a glass and there's something in it!

Today, when I work with clients in goal-setting and growing their businesses, I always encourage them to consider their values and goals for their personal lives before moving forward. I've learned and recognized in my own life that it's all interconnected. If we value time with family, we might make different choices for how to move forward than someone who is solely focused on their business or career goals. Trying to do it all and have it all is a recipe for disaster in terms of health and relationships that matter. Sometimes re-examining and redefining our definition of success leads us to what we've wanted all along.

Life doesn't always go how we think it should or planned it would, but that can be a good thing. My philosophy is that I never lose. I either win or I learn. The bombshells and challenges in life suck when you're going through them, but they serve a purpose. It all comes down to attitude and mindset. The unexpected twists, turns, and bombshells that threaten to derail us can actually change us for the better. Bombshells really can turn into blessings, if we choose to be grateful and look for the lessons within.

Cathy Sexton: Turning Bombshells Into Blessings

Cathy Sexton knows what it's like to feel stressed, overwhelmed and burned out by trying to have it all. She's lived it! And when she faced a life-threatening illness because of that lifestyle, she knew something needed to change. What changed for Cathy became not only the foundation for The Productivity Experts, but solutions and much-needed help for others still living with the struggle.

As a Productivity and Profit Specialist, speaker, author and coach, Cathy has made it her mission to help others IGNITE their productivity and streamline their lives. With a focus on understanding a person's *Natural Productivity Style* and working within it, Cathy provides actionable, easily-implemented strategies that translate to the real world and real life. She teaches people how to take control of their thoughts, incorporate systems and processes, and find the tools that work for them, so they can create a more balanced, productive life they love, while increasing profits.

Cathy is the author of *52 Powerful Success Strategies to Ignite Productivity* and a member of the National Speakers Association (NSA), The Network for Productivity Excellence, the National Chapter of Association of Professional Organizers (NAPO), NAPO St. Louis Chapter, and the local chapter of American Society of Training and Development (ASTD).

Continued...

Cathy Sexton
314-267-3969
cathy@TheProductivityExperts.com
www.TheProductivityExperts.com

https://twitter.com/cathysexton
www.youtube.com/user/CathySexton
www.facebook.com/CathySextonProductivity/
www.instagram.com/cathyasexton/

DR. JULIE STEINHAUER

Vision for Life

One thing I know, when you are trying to level up in life and business, everything will go against you. In fact, you can expect everything AND the kitchen sink to be thrown your way. Just know adversity, struggles, challenges and trials will come. This is how it's been throughout my journey as I took my dreams and turned them into reality. However, what I have learned over the years is to face my fears and level up anyway.

Sixteen years ago I dreamed of owning my own vision clinic making my part of the world a better place through vision care; a place where I would serve the masses through a positive attitude, humble heart and compassionate care. But having just graduated and not knowing really where I fit in, I went to work for a senior doctor to get some experience. A year into being a doctor I realized that I needed to open my own clinic. Working for someone else, wasn't ideally what I wanted to be doing. So, I hired the best talent to organize my clinic aesthetically so that I was on target to come out of the gate swinging and gain massive momentum. I even hired a business coach and flew him out to train me on marketing and advertising of my specialty: vision development. Jersey Family Vision Care was a reality.

Quickly reality hit. I didn't really know how to run a business. I didn't know how to make payroll when the bills were greater than the incoming funds. I didn't know how to manage the people who would come in and out of my doors as employees. In fact, if I'm being honest, I didn't know how to manage myself for success.

For nine years, I managed a vision clinic with the idea that it was a service to people and that I didn't care if I made money. I was doing my work for a bigger cause.

I was doing Kingdom work. For nine years it was a rollercoaster of ups and downs. But miraculously we survived and I managed to help many patients see better and many children gain success in the classroom for the first time in their lives through vision development and retraining their brains to process vision more efficiently.

And then it happened. I woke up one day and realized I didn't really like what I was doing. I say woke up, but I don't mean that I popped out of bed and came to that realization. I was sitting in a meeting, supporting a friend and colleague when it hit me. I realized I hated dealing with eye disease, contact lenses, and glasses! The only thing I really loved was my specialty work helping children through vision therapy to unlock their God given talent for succeeding in school!

That very same friend and colleague, whom I had gone to support that critical night, had been telling me for years that I should be focusing on my specialty. He graduated optometry school a business man. It ran through his veins. My veins had gardens, books, crafts, and a farm girl mentality to them. The day I told him I was finally ready to leave my jack-of-all-trades clinic behind and open a specialty clinic was the day he must have celebrated with a victory dance!

So I did just that. I closed my clinic and I moved to a new location, renaming my business, Vision For Life. We were a functional and developmental vision clinic. Kids, kids, and more kids, with some adults thrown in there for variety. I was on cloud nine. I knew this was what I was intended to do.

That first year in business at my new location, I had the good fortune of meeting a marketing guru. I will never forget the day she gave me a withering look. It was at my office and we had just completed making a few videos to put on YouTube. This was a scary thing by the way. No one was really utilizing YouTube back then and I ran the risk of upsetting my colleagues for sharing tips of the trade…for FREE! It was like giving the keys to the kingdom away. What if everyone stayed home and treated their own vision issues because I had shared too much information?

My marketing guru and friend, Danelle Brown of Queen Bee, thought it was a great idea to de-bunk what actually was behind vision therapy. She suggested we tell people what vision therapy was and how it worked. Monthly, we shot three, 2-minute video segments and posted to YouTube to spread the word about what I did at Vision For Life.

When I mentioned to Danelle my intentions of being a vision guru for a population in a three hour radius, my blood pumping, my excitement visible, I was clearly innergized, she said, "Julie, you want to be the guru for the world."

Gulp. How was that even possible? To be honest, it seemed like crazy talk. I had no idea over the course of the next four years that I would find out how it was very possible.

In the meantime, life happened, the toll was heavy, and I ended up going through a divorce. The next year was a year of drama. I was a single mom raising two small children, ages 4 and 2 at the time. My head was focused on anything but business. And I really didn't know how to make a business successful anyway. As you can imagine, the roller coaster ride was up and down.

Oddly enough, something came into my life the following year that I never thought would ever enter my life… and the impact it made on me was tremendous. I was introduced to another stream of income. I never imagined that I would own more than one business, as one was quite enough. But suddenly I found myself the proud owner of a home-based business. Now, I could say I had multiple businesses!

My vision business was floundering but in the meantime I was working my home-based business and I was receiving training from BIG thinkers. People who out thought ME in dreams and VISION! Don't get me wrong, I always knew I was made for more. It's hard to describe really, but when you know that you have a higher calling in life…it comes from INSIDE. These big thinkers were helping me understand that the missing link to my business taking off was me. The reality was that my business really could be getting worldwide attention.

Somehow, a switch had been flipped. Maybe it occurred when I started telling people I owned more than one business. It was strange really but just saying that statement made me FEEL like a business woman for the first time in my career. Other people must have felt this new energy as I was being taken more seriously. What occurred next was absolutely surreal.

It was odd how it happened really. I can't even recall what my thoughts were when I finally started realizing that people were beginning to contact me from all over the world. Africa, India, Great Britain, Japan and then of course people closer to home began emailing me; Canada and various states throughout the United States.

Suddenly, I was worldwide.

It really had been my mindset of thinking too small all of those years that kept me where I was. As I continued to surround myself with innovators and world changers, people who knew they were meant to do great things in the world and they were as dedicated to doing it as I was, I transformed.

It didn't come natural to me, but I was reborn into a business person. I couldn't get enough knowledge fast enough. I wanted to read every entrepreneurial book I could get my hands on. I read inspirational, motivational, and positive books to continue to upgrade my mindset. I also took a hard look at my life and who I was surrounding myself with. When you want to be a massive success, you have to pay close attention to everything, including relationships.

In 2016, we doubled the size of our clinic. On our original move I dreamed that my clinic would fill the full 3000 square feet that I had asked to be divided up for a smaller clinic. Now, it was a reality. I have room to grow and continue to build something even larger than I ever really imagined possible.

Vision for Life specializes in vision development. We train the brain to use both eyes together more efficiently and accurately, which assists our patients in all aspects of their lives. We work with children who have a variety of challenges including vision problems such as eye turns (strabismus) or lazy eye (amblyopia), reading and learning disabilities, behavior disorders, ADHD, and Autism. We also help improve eye hand and body coordination for playing sports, writing, riding a bike, and tying shoes. And we work with adult patients who want to improve driving, play a sport, reading, and enhance performance on a job. Lastly, we work with individuals who have suffered traumatic brain injury, stroke, or debilitating vision loss.

To date, as I have opened my mind to possibilities, many other exciting adventures in business have come my way. I am now coaching and mentoring women online how to be successful not only in business, but in life. I have had speaking engagements as a motivational speaker, have several books in the works, and I am more innergized than I have ever been in life! At 42 years of age, I know…never give up on your dreams. Never be afraid to dream BIG. And when you dream big…10x it! Level up and be consistent with your vision. Your vision is your life.

Dr. Julie Steinhauer: Vision for Life

Dr. Julie Steinhauer. If you were to visit Dr. Steinhauer during a vision therapy session with one of her patients, it does not take long for you to realize she is passionate about working with children. Her shoes come off, she crawls on the floor, and she often races her young patients down the hallway to the VT room!

In 2000 Dr. Steinhauer entered her last year of Optometry School at the University of Missouri St. Louis, prepared to join a practice that focused solely on eye disease management when she realized her true passion always has, and always would lie in working with children. It was during this time that she began traveling and shadowing other optometrist's vision therapy practices, in hopes that she would one day add therapy to her practice.

Before opening Vision For Life, Dr. Steinhauer owned and operated Jersey Family Vision Care in Jerseyville, IL for 9 years. In 2011 she decided to close that practice and focus solely on providing developmental vision care to the greater Edwardsville area. Vision For Life opened in April 2012 and doubled in size in June 2016.

Dr. Steinhauer is a developmental optometrist specializing in vision related learning problems, reading problems, computer vision syndrome, sports vision, and rehabilitative optometry. She is board certified in vision development as a Fellow of the College of Optometrists in Vision Development.

Dr. Steinhauer is a member of the Illinois Optometric Association, American Optometric Association, College of Optometrists in Vision Development, Optometric Extension Program, the College of Syntonic Optometry, and the Neuro-Optometric Rehabilitation Association. In addition to being President &

Continued...

CEO at Vision For Life, she is President of SWIOS - Southwestern IL Optometric Society, is a Coach and Mentor for Optometrists and Vision Therapists, runs multiple businesses online, and serves as a Coach and Mentor to online marketers.

Dr. Steinhauer has two amazing children, Emma and Ethan, who are sweet, silly, and sassy budding entrepreneurs even at their young ages. In her spare time Dr. Steinhauer enjoys reading, gardening, hiking, playing cards, traveling, baking, decorating, and business building. Her true passion is helping other people shift their mindset, dream, and work towards financial and time freedom by casting a vision, setting goals, and developing action plans to dramatically improve their lives!

Julie Steinhauer, OD, FCOVD, President
618-288-1489
drjulie@VisionForLifeWorks.com
www.VisionForLifeWorks.com

www.facebook.com/VisionForLifeWorks/
https://twitter.com/Vision4LifeWks
www.youtube.com/channel/UCEYWLm6vb_82XY_kXEriXtw

2220 S State Rte 157, Suite 350
Glen Carbon, IL 62034

KAREN O. DRAKE

Finding Life's Balance

I've always been intrigued by my Libra Zodiac sign (the scales) and because my own life journey has often been rocky, filled with twists, turns, and unpredictability, I grew up wanting to help others find balance. Balance...what does that mean? How does it show up? How does it feel? How do you get it? Over the years, I've learned to RE-view, RE-frame and RE-energize to find my balance.

RE-view. As a child, I was a military dependent, and often the "new kid in class." I needed to quickly assess the lay of the land (what type of teacher, culture of the classroom, how to fit in without losing my flavor). I also grew up with mental illness in my family, (chaos, and unpredictability) which probably fueled my desire to control or "fix" things. As a result, l learned that while I can't control anything but myself, I'm pretty good at detecting and communicating what's "unsaid/unspoken" in others and the true feelings behind that. My passion for helping others refined my academic focus and launched my early career in the helping professions.

While I've experienced some successes in life, I've also been divorced, raised two sons as a single parent, was close to filing bankruptcy twice, and was laid off with two kids in college. Life was never balanced, and I wasn't a great planner. I was much better at conceptualizing and dreaming about the future, then crafting a solid roadmap to get there. When things didn't go as planned, I'd often function in survival mode, laser-focused on a goal (pain alleviation/disaster prevention), without thinking it through, or identifying and addressing potential obstacles that could derail. I'd just DO IT.

I was not performing optimally, and quite often found myself walking through life with a disconnect between my mind/body/spirit. While dreaming may not have cost me anything, the act of NOT planning to make dreams happen, and NOT having the willingness and commitment to implement them, DID. My self-limiting beliefs, reluctance to ask for help, and avoidance of honest feedback blocked my self-awareness, and stymied my growth. I was not growing and something needed to change.

RE-frame. I was stuck. I knew something about avoiding/ignoring one's own truth, wearing a mask, and operating in a pool of denial. Representing "well" was expected in my upbringing. As an adult, I was pretty good at not letting others see the real me—imperfections and all. Was it fear of judgment, fear of rejection? That desire to "be accepted" became a key driver in my life.

I had worked hard to obtain the right education, credentials, and experiences to position myself for success. But, being degreed and talented wasn't enough—what else, outside of me, must I do to feel balanced? I learned (mostly the hard way) that most of the secret sauce wasn't "out there," but rather, as the old spaghetti sauce commercial reminded us, "It's IN there..." inside of *me*. I knew I needed support to access my own inner strength... my own secret sauce. For me, that support became clear as I learned to let God into my life.

I began to RE-frame my own life picture through the lens of my growing personal spirituality. I took a good, hard look at my own mind/body/spirit connections, and as I connected more closely with God, I learned to recognize my own inner strength—which in turn, fed my need for a stronger spiritual connection. I was no longer just trying to "perform" and achieve, but rather, I found myself more balanced—more fully engaged with a whole-life approach to living—healthier in mind, body and spirit.

Re-energize. With this new energy, I began sharing my whole-life approach to living with my clients, resulting in even more amazing results. I'm now committed to inspire others to DREAM, DEVELOP, and DO in a more authentic way, helping them to create a life of balance and abundance.

My vision is to inspire healthy living, learning and leading for individuals, teams and organizations. We start with an honest assessment of the current state, and identify the future desired; this happens in a safe space, a nonjudgmental environment to encourage vulnerability. Discovering who we really are, and articulating what we really want happens with self-awareness, reflection, and acknowledgment that a change needs to occur.

We all get stuck at various times throughout our lives, and need someone to help us sort it all out. I often hear how much clients feel "heard" and validated when we work together, especially when I hold up the "mirror" for them. People come to me to find clarity, often learning that what blocks their blessings is *them*. I help them get "unstuck" yet hold them accountable for their goals; I challenge their thinking, and help them reframe their life picture.

As we work through the **RE-view, RE-frame, Re-energize** approach, we begin to build the vision, direction, skills, and tools needed for creating balance and positive change in our lives. We assess any below-conscious motivational patterns which may be driving performance, offering a whole-life approach through a "wellness" lens. This whole-life wellness approach allows us to assess your personal satisfaction within multiple areas of life, supporting you in your journey to whole-health.

Much like "INNERGIZED Living" we learn to own where we are and draw upon experiences which have helped to shape how (who) we've come to be. Don't get me wrong, we've all been through stuff we wish to forget. However, I've learned that many of my "critics" and "valley" experiences fueled much of my motivation to create a better future. Success helped build confidence, but surrendering to God, and coping with adversity built character, resilience, and empathy from which to assess, understand, and problem solve. It also helped me to connect with other people's pain and joy. An INNERGIZED Life includes claiming what I stand for, where my efforts are consistent with my values, and others benefit from what I do. Who once said, "If you don't know what you stand for, you'll stand for anything." At the end of the day, why bother with what one does if no one else blossoms from the efforts?

Karen O. Drake is a globally-experienced consultant and executive coach, with a reputation for innovation and creative problem solving. A skillful communicator, experienced speaker, and energetic facilitator, Karen relishes opportunities to engage diverse leaders and groups to increase their confidence, and leverage emotional intelligence, to deliver exceptional results and experience greater personal satisfaction in their lives.

Because motivation matters, identification of motivational drivers and effective use of influencing language are fundamental in her work. Her whole health approach integrates the physical, emotional, mental, and spiritual elements that help or hinder someone's growth. A people whisperer, of sorts, Karen's ability to connect with and understand others, helps put people at ease and motivates them to change.

Karen earned her Bachelor's & Master's degrees in Psychology, and is certified to administer and interpret the MBTI, Inventory for Work Attitude & Motivation (iWAM), Leadership Effectiveness Analysis (LEA 360), and the LAB Profile®; a psycho-metric instrument to understand, predict and influence behavior, which can help you decode what motivates the people you need to influence. Karen is credentialed by the International Coach Federation (ICF) and is a member of the Advisory Board of The North American Institute for Work Attitude & Motivation (iWAM).

Continued…

Karen O. Drake, MA, PCC
314-805-5552
karen@KarenODrake.com
KarenODrake.com

https://www.facebook.com/karenodrakecoach/
https://www.linkedin.com/in/karendrake/

BETH HAMMOCK

Bliss on the Go

On the way home from a sales meeting, my new manager praised me for my confidence. She went into detail about the way I look, my energy level and valuable work experience. My mood immediately improved as I responded to this unexpected display of admiration.

I am courageous, I explained. I take on situations most people wouldn't want to. I always have and always will. Why? I learned courage by moving every one to two years of my childhood. Over and over, I was the new kid. I had to prove myself to teachers, classmates and coaches. I didn't see failure as an option. Thus, I stretched myself, working hard in school, trying new sports and volunteering. Most of the time, I succeeded. Then, I got to do it all again at a new school in a different part of the country. These repeated efforts built my confidence and gave me courage.

What if I had grown up in one town and had lifelong friends? I ask myself this question often. When I compare myself to people with more geographic stability, I feel a deep longing for roots. Yet when I go inside for the source of my confidence, I know the frequent moves made me who I am today.

I am a woman who has made the most of life. I raised four children and have had several rewarding careers. I've lived in 11 states, owned six houses and made friends around the world without leaving the United States. I'm physically active. I learned to ski at age 48 and now can tackle most mountains. I've practiced yoga and meditated for ten years. I celebrate my 55th birthday this week and feel fantastic.

My life hasn't always been a bed of roses. At 37, I was a divorced mother of four including three-year-old twin boys. My older children were aged 12 and 9.

The divorce was devastating for them. That was tough, but I was grateful for the release from my burden.

My kids' father and I had married in college. As devout Catholics, we saw marriage as our next right step. I quickly found out he had anger issues. He broke my tennis racket in one fight during our first six months of marriage. I knew I had made a mistake. But I stayed in the marriage for 16 years because I believed God wanted us to stay married forever. I don't believe that anymore. I believe God wants us to love one another and love ourselves. Staying with a man who was verbally abusive was not loving myself. I finally got the courage to leave when he locked himself in the bedroom all day on Christmas because he was upset about something my dad said to him. A friend said I had a long rope and it finally broke.

My ability to take care of myself financially had a significant impact on my ability to leave my husband. For the first 12 years of my career, I was a television news producer. Not only is this career super-stressful, it is relatively low-paying. After the twins were born, I quit my producing job at WDAF-TV in Kansas City to care for my kids full-time. The twins were almost three when a friend called to ask if I wanted to work in public relations for the Kansas City School District. I jumped at the opportunity. The position paid well so I could afford day care. And I felt passionate about the mission of helping inner-city children learn.

One phone call from a friend had ignited my new career in public relations. Breaks like this are a notable part of my journey. By following friends' invitations and my intuition I have moved almost effortlessly from one position to the next.

"Luck is what happens when preparation meets opportunity," the Roman philosopher Seneca said. I prepared for my TV news career by attending the Missouri School of Journalism. When I began working in PR, I attended state and national conferences. I eventually became president of the Missouri School Public Relations Association. I studied for a year for the exam to become accredited in public relations. Having that credential boosted my confidence and increased my stature in the field.

The third phase of my career began in 2005, when I landed a development position at the University of Missouri, Columbia, my alma mater. The university was in the midst of a $1 billion campaign. I had the honor of recognizing million-dollar donors with parties, media placements and publications. My manager, Linda L'Hote, taught me everything she knew. A dozen years later, I continue to be challenged and motivated in the development field. Today, I own Beth Hammock Philanthropy, a Kansas City-based consultancy helping nonprofits raise additional funds for their missions. I'm paying it forward—teaching leaders what I know about development, marketing and communications.

Now that my kids are grown, I look back and wonder how in the world I juggled demanding jobs and raising good kids. I give credit to the Innergized Life. Through yoga, prayer and meditation, I stay connected to God. I have access to the power of God anytime, anywhere. God is so many qualities, including love, wisdom, joy and prosperity. Knowing I am a living display of these qualities helps me show up in a positive way wherever I am called.

I have always felt close to God. My parents took us to mass every Sunday. By the time I was in high school, I was a lector, teaching Sunday school and leading retreats. When I got divorced, my husband and I had been presenting Marriage Encounter weekends for three years. I valued marriage, but not enough to stay in a bad one. Continuing in the Catholic Church was difficult for me because I felt guilty every time I went. I was supposed to have stayed married, I thought.

My counselor suggested I try Unity. My first experience with Unity was at Unity Temple on the Plaza, the Unity movement's flagship church. I cried then and at many Sunday services thereafter. I was crying for both joy and in grief, letting go of my relationship with Catholicism.

Unity recommends meditating daily. Adopting this practice changed my life. I can settle my anxious mind and find a place of peace through meditation. I often hear God speaking to me when my mind is clear. Love wells up inside me and I am prepared for whatever comes my way.

At the suggestion of my brother, Dr. David Kearney, I added yoga to my self-care practices. David's research is about the impact of meditation and mindfulness training on patients with post-traumatic stress disorder. He recommended I take a Mindfulness-based Stress Reduction class, so I did. This class gave me a foundation for using yoga and meditation for creating more peace in my life. It works.

I'm a firm believer in re-creation—getting out of the office to give myself time to think. I have a lot of my best ideas while walking my dog. A daily connection with nature is a must for me.

When I travel, either for work or to visit my children, I seek out the most beautiful place around and spend some time there. For example, when I flew to Spokane, Washington to watch my son play college football, I gave myself four days for the trip—two for travel, one for watching the game and one for me. Immediately after arriving, I went to Anthony's, a seafood restaurant perched above Spokane Falls. I indulged in three of my favorite foods: salmon, peaches and raspberries on a salad. Then I sat there and worked for a couple of hours. I chatted with the staff and felt right at home.

After my visit to Anthony's, I wandered along the river and came upon a food truck festival. Since I had just eaten, I relaxed by getting a chair massage. Then, it was off to Sandpoint, Idaho, about an hour northeast of Spokane. I had been to Sandpoint once before and fell in love with its sandy beach and mountain views. My Airbnb host was surprised I had just one day for the visit. Being content with a one-day retreat is an essential component of my Innergized Life. The highlight of my visit was practicing yoga on the water's edge on a perfect day. Blissful moments like this re-charge me.

I have written this chapter one day after moving from St. Louis to Kansas City. I am surrounded by boxes and one may think my life is in disarray. I know it is in perfect order. Three months ago, I hung photos of peonies on the walls of my new apartment in St. Louis. Six weeks later, I received an offer to work with Powell Gardens, Kansas City's botanical garden. I decided to move back to help raise more money for Powell Gardens. I visualized being surrounded by flowers and now I am.

Beth Hammock: Bliss on the Go

As the founder of Beth Hammock Philanthropy, **Beth Hammock** helps nonprofit organizations raise more money for their missions. She advises leaders on fundraising campaigns and creates compelling campaign collateral including publications, websites and videos. In addition to her career success, Beth raised four children as a single mom.

Beth began her career as a TV news producer. When her family doubled with the birth of twins in 1996, she changed careers and began working in public relations. She served in PR roles for several large, high profile organizations including the Kansas City School District, the Missouri Attorney General's Office and the University of Missouri, Columbia. From 2010 to 2014, Beth was vice president, strategic communications and marketing for the University of Montana Foundation in Missoula, Montana.

Beth returned to Missouri in 2014 to serve as editor of *Daily Word* magazine. She has edited several spiritual books and is a guest speaker at Unity churches.

Beth's client list includes Powell Gardens, Kansas City's botanical garden, the UMKC Foundation, UMKC Honors College, University of Central Missouri Alumni Foundation, University of Alaska Fairbanks, University of Alaska Foundation, and the International Brotherhood of Magicians.

Continued...

Beth Hammock
314-896-4341
beth@BethHammock.com
www.BethHammock.com

www.facebook.com/beth.hammock
www.linkedin.com/in/bethhammock1/
www.instagram.com/beth.hammock/
https://twitter.com/BethHammock5

JEANNIE KRAUSE-TAYLOR

"Like Mother, Like Daughter"
Proverb

Mirror, mirror on the Wall… **"I am my mother after all"**!! This is the tip of the iceberg when describing the mother-daughter relationship—the most complex relationship in a family.

Over the years, I have listened to numerous adult daughters who were my clients, caring for their aging parents, and to friends and family members talking about the trials and tribulations of their relationships with their mothers. During many a night out with "the girls", our dinner conversations evolved from issues with children and spouses, to mother-daughter concerns. I began to hear common themes of frustration, stress, and worry about caring for aging mothers.

My first insights into this complex relationship came from watching my mother care for her mother. Grandma had two children, a son and a daughter. My parents lived just a few miles from my grandmother, while her son lived 35 miles away. As Grandma aged, my mother, Bonnie began helping her more, taking her shopping, and accompanying her to medical appointments, while my father mowed her yard and was her personal handyman. Later when Grandma moved into assisted living and eventually a nursing facility, my mother continued her caregiving duties, doing laundry and collaborating with the staff and physician. Meanwhile my mother's brother, George would take Grandma out to lunch—once a week. Grandma was very appreciative of his visits and would "sing his praises" to my mother. Meanwhile my mother would vent her frustrations to my sister and I that she received little acknowledgment for her efforts and felt that Grandma "expects" her to take care of everything, while having few expectations of her brother.

This story stayed with me over the years, and after I began my business, Pathways for Aging, I would think of it often, as the caregiving daughters who called, would tell me their stories. Having seen the difference in expectations a mother can have between a daughter and a son, in my own family, enabled me to better understand what they were going through. Not all the stories were the same, but I began to see a theme. I began asking the daughters about their relationship with their mother prior to caregiving. Many reported poor to fair relationships. I recall one daughter declaring "there is a reason I moved across the country after graduating college—to get away from my mother. As long as we visited just a few times a year, things were fine, but now that I need to be more involved…"

This seems to be the exclamation of many women hitting that stage of life, when we find ourselves caring for aging parents. When I think of all the women I have met with over the years, I hear this common refrain "My mother is making me crazy!"

What happens when an adult daughter begins to care for her aging mother? It varies, depending on the relationship that has been developed over their lifetime. Has it been a relationship of caring or criticism? The history of the relationship may make the reversal of their roles more challenging, ranging from great love and respect—to a mix of resentment, guilt, and anger. As women age, the relationship changes when new demands are placed on the daughter, and the mother is forced to relinquish her power; roles begin to reverse and the balance of power shifts.

Several years ago, I was teaching at a local university and while researching articles for my class, I began researching the literature about relationships between adult daughters and their mothers. I was curious, was what I had been hearing, supported by research? I learned that researchers had already begun to investigate the complexities of the mother-daughter relationship. My experiences and theories were confirmed. In fact, researchers report that Mothers and Daughters have the most complex relationship in the family, and that this relationship can be a source of great comfort and great pain to each of them

What makes the relationship between mother and daughter such a special bond, yet can also make it so stressful? It is emotionally charged, and we push each other's *buttons* so easily. A remark coming from your mother can be more healing or hurtful, than the same remark coming from someone else. Women have invested much into this relationship; both the mother and the daughter. It is one of the most passionate relationships in a woman's life. It can be the source of the deepest love, anger, and even hate that most women experience. It impacts how we relate to others, both within and outside of our families.

There can be anger and resentment on both sides. Recently I told one of my clients, 85-year-old Margaret, I was writing this article. She lives in an exclusive senior citizens residence, but is so angry that her daughter made the decision to sell her home that they seldom speak. She was very intrigued and said, "This is what you should include in your article, mothers care for their children throughout childhood and often until they complete college, but when the mother needs help, they do not take her into their home, instead putting her in a place like this."

There are also mothers and daughters who appear to handle caregiving effortlessly. I recall one client, Delores, who had two daughters, who lived out-of-state. They flew into town when a crisis arose and hired me to provide care management for their mother after they left. I accompanied their mother to medical appointments and assisted the family in locating a reliable home care company which began caring for their mother in her home. Both daughters said their goal was to relocate their mother closer to one of them. All three had a very loving relationship. The daughters both spoke fondly of their mother and reported a good relationship with her throughout their lives.

As a professional caregiver, hearing countless stories from my caregiving clients, as well as from their mothers, I have come to recognize that *aging is a family affair*, and frequently I spend as much or more time coaching caregivers as I do providing services with the parents/loved ones for whom they care. Caregivers often need support and guidance in ways to better manage their relationship and to be taught skills to enhance communication and coached in setting boundaries. I assist them in deciding what tasks and roles only they can fulfill and what they can delegate to other family members or paid help. A family meeting facilitated by a professional can help other family members better understand the stresses and burdens of the designated caregiver.

I can recall that on two occasions I facilitated meetings where sons appeared to finally hear their sisters, and volunteered to become more involved in providing care for their mothers. At the conclusion of the meeting, John volunteered to accompany his sister and their mother to medical appointments, so she could have some support and assistance. Tom agreed to begin helping with household chores and meals when it was his turn to visit his parents, and not just have a social visit. In both situations the daughters reported that the increased help and support of their sibling, eased their stress and they no longer needed my services!

Frequently my focus is on educating adult daughters, and sons, helping them understand the changes their mothers are experiencing, and how they impact the changes in their relationship. Through my work as President of Pathways for Aging, I have learned much about the impact of aging on each of us. Through assisting families to manage their struggles in changing family roles, I have found they can improve their relationships as they understand the need to respect and appreciate each other, which helps improve communication skills. Families may also need to learn techniques to decrease stress as roles continue to change. Mothers may need coaching, as I work with them to help them accept their need for care and to graciously accept offers for assistance from their well-meaning daughters.

Often I am told how much I look like my mother. I too have looked in the "mirror" and I am my mother after all! My Grandmother passed away many years ago, and now it is my sister and I who are caring for our mother. She lives in an apartment in a senior complex and still cares for herself, but we oversee medical care and her finances. As she ages, our duties increase. Fortunately we had a great relationship with our mother throughout our lives, which facilitates our relationship now that our roles are reversing. Recently my mother said to me "Isn't it funny, I took care of you all those years and now you are taking care of me?" It was a touching moment and reminds me that life is full circle, and how fortunate I am to have such a great relationship with my mother.

My passion is to assist women to have richer and more fulfilling relationships with their mothers and daughters.

Jeannie Krause-Taylor, MSW, LCSW, C-ASWCM founded Pathways for Aging in 2004 after more than 20 years of experience as a professional social worker because, she has seen the strain, frustration, and feelings of helplessness experienced by older adults, families and caregivers as they struggle with difficult changes in their roles and life-altering decisions related to aging.

Jeannie's previous experience includes serving as the Social Work Manager for Barnes-Jewish Hospital, and Case Manager Supervisor with the St. Louis Regional Center for the Developmentally Disabled. Jeannie has also served as an Adjunct Faculty Member at Washington University in Saint Louis, where she instructed social work students seeking their Master's Degree.

Active in the community and with professional organizations, Jeannie is the Past-President of the Board of Directors for Housing Options Provided for the Elderly (HOPE), and has served as an officer on the Board of the Gateway Chapter of the Older Women's League (OWL). She is also an Advanced Professional Member of the Aging Life Care Association (ALCA), and a member of the National Association of Social Workers (NASW). She served several terms on the Board of Directors for the Missouri Chapter of NASW.

Continued...

Jeannie Krause-Taylor
314-395-7560
j.krausetaylor@PathwaysForAging.com
www.PathwaysForAging.com

https://www.linkedin.com/in/jeannie-krause-taylor-56552b9/
https://www.facebook.com/PathwaysForAging/
Pathways4Aging@Twitter.com

11628 Old Ballas Road, Suite 331
Saint Louis, MO 63141

KELLY DEROSSETT

A Blank Canvas

Full of excitement heading to San Diego for a seminar designed to create absolute wealth, I was in line to board the plane when a colleague I rarely spoke with popped up on my caller ID. Curious as to why Carol would be calling, I answered. "Well, we didn't know if we should call and tell you or not, but, First Magnus just filed bankruptcy." I'm not exactly sure what I said to Carol, I think I thanked her for the call and assured her I was glad she let me know. I was numb. Two weeks earlier to the day our former employer, American Home Mortgage, had filed bankruptcy. Stunned, I thought, "Two different employers had filed bankruptcy just two weeks apart?" As I boarded the plane, still in a state of shock, I determined the universe had just handed me a blank canvas to create my absolute wealth. I am a true self-help seminar junkie and this weekend didn't let me down. It was awesome and I came back home with the start of a game plan to begin my exit from the mortgage industry that was imploding around me.

My path has had some twists and turns along the way, as I am sure yours has as well. After my exit from the mortgage industry I have had the opportunity to coach, consultant and work as a national professional speaker and corporate trainer. These experiences have allowed me to create a business and lifestyle that works for my family.

Today I run Activate Social Media, a boutique social media and marketing firm that focuses on assisting sales professionals and small businesses create and execute marketing plans to increase brand awareness and sales. And I love it! Ten years ago, I would not have even been able to imagine owning my own business, let alone loving my work as I help others achieve their goals. When I chose to open my social media and marketing firm I had two foundational pieces: make marketing affordable to businesses at all levels and deliver what I promise. Many business owners I had met over the years felt marketing was too expensive or they had not received the value the marketer had promised. I wanted to create marketing that was authentic and affordable.

As a social media strategist, I will share a few pointers to help you create your INNERgized life:

Step 1: Assessment. Where are you right now? Taking the time to have an honest look at what is working and what is not working and WHY is a great first step toward achieving your mission. When I met my wife, I was travelling the country as a national speaker and loved it. I felt energized everyday as I shared information and resources to help others help themselves. Once my wife and I became serious, being on the road three to four weeks a month was not working. This led me to the next step.

Step 2: Visualize. What do you want? Get as detailed as possible. Make lists of what you want and what you don't want. What you like and what you don't like. Do you work for yourself or someone else? Do you work at home, in an office or on the road? What do you love to do? What are you great at? What is not your forte? Think about this from a work/life balance perspective. As I created my next step after retiring from my road warrior days it was important to me to have a flexible schedule. My wife works overnights as an ER nurse. I wanted to be able to work when she was at work. Creating an online business where I work from home was a perfect fit for me. I had learned from my time traveling that the desire for marketing services was needed. Organizations were challenged by technology, time or marketing expertise. Recognizing that I had a skill to offer, I invested in an online course. Combining what I had learned over the years as a coach and consultant I was able to design, actually visualize, a social media agency. Two of my favorite books helped me get clear on my strengths: The Passion Test by Chris & Janet Attwood and Strength Finder by Tom Rath. Rath explains, "When you work from your strengths, it makes work easier and enjoyable."

Step 3: Profit & Passion Plan. Now that you know what you want, create a plan to produce profits from your passion(s). Remember to include, specific measurable goals and action steps. One of the first steps I walk clients through is monthly cash flow. You need to know what monthly income your business must generate to be a viable income source. We discuss savings, alternative income sources and the new business costs that will be incurred. This gives us a timeframe and lays the groundwork to move forward on action steps.

Although it may sound cliché, when your work is what you love to do, it doesn't feel like work. Create your INNERgized life by combining your passions, skills, strengths and talents to create income streams. You could be self-employed or work for someone else. Use the internet to discover how others are combining their time & talent to create income. Many find this step challenging. In my consulting practice I offer an activation session to help you discover and synthesis a plan of action to create profits from your passion. As strange as this may sound to some of you, during consultations I believe the universe is sharing information allowing me to help my clients. My ideal clients "get this".

Step 4: Press "Start". You have a plan in hand and it is time to take action. Sounds simple, right? Believe it or not, this is where many get stuck. Many of us are afraid of failing or looking stupid. If I never start, I can't fail. Wrong! Give yourself permission to fail forward. During the first year of my social media business I had one large client. I knew I needed to add more clients; I just didn't have a sense of urgency because the revenue from my one client was substantial. I did such an excellent job for that client she invested the increased sales in bringing on a full-time marketing person to execute the marketing strategy in-house. Ouch! I wasn't ready for that. On the positive side, my strategy worked-I could make it work for my own business. I determined it would be better for me to have several clients at various package levels to spread out my revenue sources. Get knocked down seven times, get up eight times.

Step 5: Evaluate & Recalculate. What went right? What could go better? Are you seeking additional training or education? Do you want a promotion? Do you want to grow or add staff? While you evaluate, consider obtaining outside perspective or assistance. If you are employed, a mentor or career coach would be able to share insight and feedback. Business owners may want to consider a coach, consultant or peer roundtable. One of the best business tips I ever heard was "First Friday". The first Friday of every month evaluate the results of the previous month. Check-in and see if your results are meeting or exceeding your goals. What do you need to continue and discontinue to stay on track to recalculate? What do you need to do in the next 30 days to move forward?

Step 6: Accountability. Create a system to stay accountable. Peer roundtable, coach, mentor, consultant, Facebook group, online membership group or all the above. Depending on your situation you can determine what would work best for you. Solopreneurs may find maintaining motivation particularly challenging. Staying accountable is also one of my challenges as a business owner. I have a few things that work for me to stay on track and accountable. I have an online group that facilitates "accountability buddies" and has scheduled check-ins. I also have a local community of business women that sponsor live events promoting connectedness, motivation and goal setting. Find what works for you and be accountable to yourself.

Step 7: Keep learning. More than ever in today's age of technology it is important to stay up to date. I am convinced my commitment to lifelong learning has been pivotal as I navigated the many twists and turns of my career path. Having a wide knowledge base and up to date skills allows you to reinvent yourself as the economy and technology changes. I easily spend 10 to 20 hours a week learning and studying social media, marketing, and current trends. This is the competitive edge I offer my clients in order to coordinate and execute their marketing strategy.

Congratulations on your desire to move forward toward creating a life fueled by your passions. I am confident when you implement these pointers you will be well on your way to creating your own success story. I am eager to hear about your INNERgized life. What was your favorite tip? What challenges are you facing? Feel free to contact me at Kelly@ActivateSocialMedia.com with any questions or comments you may have.

Providing Affordable & Effective Social Media Solutions
to Execute your Business Goals

Kelly DeRossett: A Blank Canvas

Kelly DeRossett is a proud lifelong St. Louis native. She graduated the University of Missouri-Columbia with a dual degree in Marketing & Business Logistics. She proceeded to work in a variety of industries in sales and marketing earning multiple awards & recognition for outstanding sales and customer satisfaction. Passionate about sharing her knowledge with others Kelly traveled the country as a national speaker. When love knocked and wedding bells rang she retired off the road and founded Activate Social Media in 2014. As a boutique social media and marketing firm Kelly provides clients with marketing strategies that align with their business goals. Kelly and her wife, Jonnie, enjoy traveling and have a bucket list (partially complete) full of adventures near & far. The family is complete with four children & one very spoiled dachshund, Maddie.

Kelly DeRossett
314-322-8322
kelly@ActivateSocialMedia.com
www.ActivateSocialMedia.com

www.facebook.com/activatesocialmedia/?ref=bookmarks
https://twitter.com/activatesocmed
www.linkedin.com/in/activatesocialmedia/
www.pinterest.com/KellyAlcorn/
plus.google.com/b/108431063316232475315/+The
  BusinessActivationCoachFenton

PAT POWERS

Finding My Inner Child

My Inner Child became so excited to share the long journey of healing and allowing the Light of an unfettered soul to shine through. When the idea of writing about an "inner" journey came up, I had to ask myself which of the wonderful manifestations I would share. My thoughts began to race with creative ideas—my long-term marriage of 35 plus years is extra-ordinary. My journey through ministerial school achieving my Master's Degree at age 50 was pretty extra-ordinary. Maybe I would write about my recent breast cancer experience, which taught me how dark a tunnel of depression can become, and how to take the next right step to healing—also, pretty interesting and extra-ordinary. Really, none of these things would have come about in my life without the unfolding of my whole life, the good, the bad and the beautiful.

I began (literally) one St. Patrick's Day when my father, a Navy man, happened to be on leave and at home with my mom. Being an Irishman—after a pint or two—a little surprise was created. My spirit, a little Soul from Heaven, came in to Being. I think we come into the life we have for a Divine reason. My lessons to learn were already in alignment to ultimately serve my highest good. Nine months later, my Mother gave birth to me: Patricia Ann Powers. I arrived home Christmas morning. Susan, the older sister by six years was not happy to meet a baby. She really wanted a puppy and told everyone she was not happy.

From the beginning, it was pretty rough. Mother and Father divorced when I was 4. He did not call, or write, or see us. I was only four, my sister was 10. She knew her daddy and remembered him. I soon forgot. My little brother Charlie was born 4 months after my mother married my step-dad. And it began. Charles, a narcissist concerned only about feeding his own desires. My older sister was first. She believed that by being the target she was saving me from the nightmare of sexual abuse. She finally could take no more and ran away at 17. She had not been saving me. The manipulation, control and secrets began before kindergarten.

As a child, being taught about secrets and how important it was to keep them was demonstrated many times over my young years. The most impactful happened when my step-dad took our dog, King, away. He told me that if I ever told anyone what he was doing with me, he would do the same to my baby brother. These are very scary threats for a little girl to understand. So, I began to protect myself from what was happening. I learned that my spirit was safe when I pulled her into my heart. I boxed that innocence in, and began brick by brick to build a wall to keep her safe.

I learned to "keep 'em laughing" by being the center of attention. I learned to walk on eggshells when the effects of the alcohol started to come out. I would tuck that part of me that needed protection in the box, within my heart, behind the brick wall. The Patty I let people see was the strong, outgoing, overachiever, always happy, always diverting attention. Keeping secrets.

Physical abuse within our home included inserting his fingers in my sister's mouth and pulling until he ripped her cheeks. Why? She smiled. Charles came in from a union meeting; drunk and threatening to shoot us all. All three children and Mom were lined up on the sofa, and this mad-man proceeded to rant and rave with a pistol in hands, threatening to shoot us. Another brick in the wall. Mother had an occasional black eye from bumping into a cabinet door—a few too many times. Secrets, covering with lies, were more bricks in my wall. We were beaten with a belt till we had welts and bruises and could not tell, another secret, another brick. Far too many abuses or stories to tell.

As I matured and grew up, I had learned to hide my light, to be in relationships where I was manipulated and controlled because it was familiar. I dated people who were older, emotionally unavailable and abusive. Yes, I was a very submissive people pleaser, like my mother, with a man who was like my step-dad. Abusers abuse. Abused people often go back to the same types of situations, or worse.

My Inner journey to heal the trauma Little Patty experienced has taken many years, and brought me a long way. Many teachers and facilitators assisted in my setting my Inner Child free. It felt like when all the bad things happened, and when that little spirit would feel fear, she would disappear. My spirit would tuck itself away in a little box, inside of me. A stronger Outer Patty would jump up to protect my inner child, my soul.

This stronger Patty would speak up, distract with jokes and antics. This one was a bit loud, a bit outrageous. This one showed off the talent to be the center of attention, to act as everyone expected. All the while, the Inner me was stuck, tucked away. Not allowed to shine because of fear, the wall expanded around the small box within me which contained her. My mental chatter let me know loud and clear that I was mentally ill. I felt as if I had two personalities like Sybil (a movie by the same name records 17 multiple personalities). I only had two. They talked to each other, convincing me I was not like anyone else. I kept the idea I was diagnosable to myself, just another secret.

Always keeping secrets. I was still missing something. Now I understand that missing piece was the "unbroken" "innocent" "authentic" self—the Truth of me; without it being hidden away in a box, walled in behind large bricks, built very high through experience after experience.

As I matured and life moved on, I married my Champion. He has dedicated his time with me to helping let my light shine, not just a little, but to its fullest! For the first decade we were busy making a living and having children. Then I discovered a Spiritual Center where I found a "faith, a philosophy, and a way of life." The Science of Mind is the textbook written by Ernest Holmes that began my transformation. Changing my thinking was really making changes in my life. I was learning that I have choice in how I live, that I am not a victim to anyone, that God is no respecter of persons. I actually had to unlearn everything I knew, most importantly, I changed my belief about God. For me, God is not a person (man in the sky who judges and is angry), but rather an energy, a power for good.

The Inner Child Workshop facilitated by Rev. Dr. Clancy Blakemore in St. Louis came to our center. For the first time ever, I felt safe to look at my story. This was a three-day intensive workshop and I knew if I was ever going to heal, now was the time. Little by little I talked about what had happened in my home. I listened as other people shared their secrets and home life.

I felt so safe I could actually confess that I felt I had two personalities and I needed help. Another minister, Rev. Phylis Clay came to talk with me. My fear was that I would be sent to an institution and never get out again if anyone really knew how messed up I was. Reverend Clay asked me a powerful question, "Do you think you have two souls?" I thought a moment and said no. She went on to point out that we have one hand; the top is very different from the bottom. I was not two separate selves; I was one whole, perfect Being.

So began my journey to wholeness.

I allowed myself to look at my abusive childhood, and see the way it had manifested as patterns of behavior in many parts of my life. Responses to situations were imprinted on me very early. After the workshop, I wrote the letter to my step-dad, and actually gave it to him. I had an honest conversation with my mother about her complicit role in what happened in our home. My sister and I were finally able to tell the truth about how we had controlled, manipulated and made to keep the family secrets secret. I was not easy, but it was necessary.

After the first weekend, there was so much opening within me. I could see how I had masked my own self in the process of just surviving till adulthood. I could see how I had learned to be subservient, and do as I was told. I realized the path to my greatest expression of good included helping others move beyond victimhood, to surviving and thriving. My experience made the perfect storm to create my calling to the ministry and to serve and now facilitate this work in the world. To date, I have participated in and facilitated in excess of 35 workshops.

Rev. Pat Powers is an Ordained Minister with the Centers for Spiritual Living. She is Spiritual Director with Contemporary Spiritual Arts, a Ministry in St. Louis Missouri.

Rev. Pat is a wedding officiate and facilitates workshops and weekend intensives, teaches classes, speaks to groups (both large and small), does personal coaching, is a fund-raiser/auctioneer, and has performed stand up comedy and sung the Blues for hundreds of conference attendees. Pat teaches a powerful, positive-thinking spiritual philosophy to the seeker, the "Cultural Creatives" who are looking for love, inspiration and fulfillment; and a way to leave the world a better place.

Pat has been married to Art Licklider for many years. They have two grown children, and three grandchildren, so far. Life is good – All the time.

The Bridges Workshop, an Inner Child Weekend is being planned for three locations a year. Please watch the website for more info.

Rev. Pat Powers
636-577-5000
revpat@RevPatPowers.com
www.RevPatPowers.com
Call for private sessions

www.facebook.com/revpatpowers

PAM WILSON

The Story Teller

Ever since I can remember I wrote stories. There hasn't ever been a time that I can remember that I wasn't writing or thinking about writing. From my earliest days I loved stories. Of all kinds. Books, movies, live theatre. I simply love a good story well told.

One of my skills is listening to anyone's ideas as well as my own and creating a story. By doing this I am able to process life and lessons in my journey. In fact, sometimes re-telling the story is so much better I wish it was my real life.

Telling stories is my way to understand my life and what I learn from others. Story-telling doesn't chase emotions away, it gives me a structure within which to grow and learn. I'm curious about people, their stories and how people think and live. By telling stories I am able to share and inspire myself and others to live the biggest, most truthful life we can.

How in the world did I end up here? How does a beach bunny end up in land-locked St. Louis, smack in the middle of suburban life telling stories?

This wasn't supposed to be my life. I dreamed of going to New York and writing for magazines, never getting married, and having lots of friends. You know—a fabulous life. Whenever I was asked, this would always be my answer. I would write, explore, travel and have adventures.

As luck, fate and the universe would have it; my path did not lead me to New York to write. Somewhere along the way, I realized I would have to be practical and support myself. I see now that I wasn't ready to write.

Enter real life.

When I finally found myself in the school where I thrived, I was working with young children and their families. I was good at it and enjoyed it, although I could barely pay my bills. Heading back to graduate school, I managed to do some writing, but still nothing of much interest.

Then a funny thing happened. Life found me. I ended up earning a Masters of Social Work degree, getting married and had kids.

And *that's* how I ended up in suburbia. At the ripe old age of 40, I took a look around and realized that there had to be something more.

There was.

When an injury sidelined me, forcing me to be still (not one of my favorite things), I began to write. I wrote about what I knew, which was raising a family and living in suburbia. And though I was always thankful for that life, I tellingly titled my column *S.O.S. From Suburbia*. For me, writing about what I knew was saving me, yet at the time I didn't realize it. I just knew I could tell stories and this helped me survive and thrive in my life.

I knew that the nuts and bolts of day to day life weren't all that interesting, so I kept writing until I was able to find my voice. With the encouragement of my Uncle Steve who continued to tell me I HAD a voice, I realized that I was emphasizing the humor in everyday aspects of life. By sharing what I was living and struggling with, I found that others were identifying with the stories and finding comfort in the knowledge that they are not alone. The same things are happening in all our households. It's *how we deal with them* that defines and ultimately shapes who we and our families are. I believe this today even more.

I wrote about the lunacy of raising kids in today's world: crazy sports coaches, even crazier moms living through their daughters, pole dancing, struggling to make dinner each night, the absence of sleep, strong women helping one another, raising a teenage boy, taming curly hair, the love of chocolate and allowing ice cream for dinner. It was all funny and clever in my head.

I realized my life was the story of a beach girl surviving suburbia while raising responsible, interesting, confident kids, running car-pool and dancing with my girlfriends. All while maintaining a sense of myself. I realized fairly late in the game that the universe knew exactly what I needed the whole time. With a few little spins (how far is the beach?) I knew I was making suburbia survivable through story-telling. The point is to juggle everything and find a balance I could live with. I do it every day. Survival doesn't have to have a negative connotation-in fact, survival strategies and how we make our lives work is quite positive. For me, it's living every day and finding all the good that makes life worthwhile.

I figured out a way to get it on paper and then I started telling people. My friend Eric gifted me with the best description of my writing: "It's like 'Sex and the City' without the sex and without the city." This, my story was and is a different story. These are stories of life here in suburbia in the middle of the country.

Mostly, I found that my stories are inspiring people; relating to the craziness that is messy, loud and real life.

Then something happened yet again. Somewhere along the way, I got lost in my life. I'm not even sure how it happened, I just know it did. R.E.M sings, "It's the end of the world and we know it. And I feel fine." Now, today, I know that it IS the end of the world as I knew it and I am more than fine.

What happened to me happens to many women. I think that I lost myself and all that was important to me in the process of trying to keep the peace, protect my kids and keep a family together.

It's taken a Tribe to remind me that I can be true to myself, rise above all the chaos and maintain a stronger sense of myself in any and all situations. I allowed pieces of myself to get lost because I thought I was doing the right thing. The result has been a journey of finding me again. Of reminding myself and coming back to the person I've been all along. A woman who possesses courage, power, strength, wisdom and wonder.

I had no idea the core of steel that resides within me but it does. That has always been inside of me. Resilience? I have that oozing out of my pores. Strength is being able to look someone in the eye and calmly say, "I disagree," without explanation or defense. It means taking the high road because when we do, we don't regret it. It means staying tough with dignity.

What does it take for any of us to DECIDE that we own our lives? That it's up to us to make it happen. Reach for the stars. Try new things. Be BRAVE. Say yes. Open ourselves up to whatever the Universe, fate, and life brings us. To define our own lives and our own joy. HOW FREAKING SCARY.

Let's be real.

Change is scary. The status quo is sometimes so much easier to maintain because the unknown is well, the unknown. But then I wondered. How much of a dis-service am I doing myself by clinging to something that doesn't work? That isn't good for me or my kids? Why is risk so scary? Why is putting ourselves out here so frightening?!

I define what happiness is: THIS is what taking responsibility of my life CAN feel like. Powerful, challenging, exciting, scary and stretching my comfort zone.

Because it's true.

I.

Am.

Responsible.

For...

MY OWN HAPPINESS. I am responsible for MY OWN STORY.

Nobody else is. Just me. I am the one that makes me happy. With my choices and decisions and actions. I have to look myself in the mirror every single day. I have to live with myself. At the end of it all, I have to know that I was kind enough. I listened enough. I did enough. I loved enough. I hugged enough. I danced enough. That I held on enough when I needed to and that yes, I let go enough when I needed to as well.

It wasn't until I began feeling differently about myself and my journey and the changes I was not only surviving but living through and with, that I realized people-friends old and new were responding to me in a way I remembered. Not only was I breathing again, I felt lighter. I felt sparkly. Here, in suburbia.

My story has always been about my time. About using the time well and living well. Now more than ever. Loving, wondering and exploring and being happy. Regardless if I'm on the beach, in suburbia or figuring out what my next courageous, powerful, wonderful journey will encompass, it's my story.

THIS is my life. Now. Every single second.

And I'm going for it with everything I've got.

To remind myself of this promise, I look at the stars every night. Catching my breath; the sky is clear and lit up with a million stars. Some winking. Some solid and true within themselves. More stars than I've seen in a while. A truly beautiful sky. This is my victory song...remembering to look up.

This is my story and I'm sticking with it.

Pam Wilson: The Story Teller

Pam Wilson is a writer, licensed Master Social Worker, Book Coach and creator/facilitator of Write ON! a community-based writing program that empowers participants to find their voice and inspire change in the world. See the work at: https://www.facebook.com/WriteONstlouis/

Her Book Coaching with Davis Creative began in January 2017; she is currently coaching three authors. She is also the Editor of the INNERgized Anthology to be published in October 2017.

For fifteen years she wrote the *S.O.S. From Suburbia* column for "St. Louis Moms and Dads," part of the *St. Louis Post-Dispatch*. The columns were about real life written in a relatable, humorous way. Find them at: http://www.stltoday.com/lifestyles/parenting.

She has written pieces that appeared in *St. Louis Magazine*/Family edition both on-line and in print. She has written the "Off the Beaten Path" column for SwimBikeRun St. Louis chronicling her adventures in out of the ordinary exercise options.

In 2012, she self-published *SOS from Suburbia*, a compilation of humorous essays which supported her belief that a well-told, entertaining story about individuality and family was welcome and needed in our common community. She put the real back into reality with commentary on everyday life.

Presently, she writes a blog about her oh-so-interesting life where she puts her unique spin on everyday happenings and the journey of being human at: https://youcallitchaosicallitlife.wordpress.com

Continued...

Pam has raised two amazing kids over the last twenty years and calls them her greatest accomplishments. She loves to bike, read, travel and hike with her dog. One day she hopes to live on or near a beach.

Previously she was a school social worker in the Special School District of St. Louis after earning a Masters of Social Work from Washington University. Her undergraduate degree is in Child and Family development from University of Missouri at Columbia.

Pam Wilson
314-853-2554
GroovyChickPJW@gmail.com
pam@DavisCreative.com
www.stltoday.com/lifestyles/parenting
https://youcallitchaosicallitlife.wordpress.com

www.facebook.com/WriteONstlouis/
www.stltoday.com/lifestyles/parenting
www.linkedin.com/in/pam-wilson-14477110a/

REV. DENISE JUDD

Unlocking the Heart

Physical challenges are often easier than emotional ones. If given the choice, we would gladly jump off a cliff into water before sharing feelings of hurt, sadness or fear. I spent some precious moments with a preteen recently who, while playing around with some other younger children, accidentally hurt one of them. The other child was fine but wanted some acknowledgment of the physical pain that was caused. The preteen had said sorry multiple times but it came with an edge where it was not believable to the other child, or to me. What would it take for this to be a genuine apology?

Having the courage to let out whatever was causing this girl to shutdown and close off. I asked this sweet hearted and usually joyful girl if she would come with me to the other room for a couple of minutes. When I asked her what was going on, she repeatedly said, "I'm fine" and yet clearly she wasn't. This is typical of all of us when we have emotions going on and are too afraid of letting them out because of the fear of being overwhelmed by them or judged for them.

After several attempts to have her share and getting the same "I'm fine" response, I leaned over and gave her a hug and told her what a huge heart she had and that I was here if she needed anything. I then placed my hand over her heart and left it there. She asked me what I was doing and I said I'm just putting my hand on your heart. This is something that I know can have a powerful effect on someone's ability to open their heart just a smidge and let things out. She asked me why I was doing that, and after searching for the right words for this 11 year old to understand, I believe I said something profound like, "just because". Lol

There were only a few seconds before tears began to pour down her face and she spoke up and said that she hurts when others hurt. The pain she was feeling that this other child got hurt was so intense that she tried to shut it off and stuff it down so as to not be judged by her sensitivity. She repeatedly told me this was normal and even though I knew she didn't believe that, I reassured her that it was indeed normal for someone who has such a huge heart like hers. I told her I understood what she was feeling and how hard it can be to feel that deeply. I shared with her a little bit of my own story and how I can get overwhelmed with the pain of others in the world going through major things like school shootings, homelessness or friends and family members going through cancer treatment or other illnesses. I shared with her that I even get a sensation that travels down my whole body when coming across an animal that has something going on in their body that maybe even the owner is unaware of. She shook her head and could relate to this as well.

I spoke to her about the gift of having a huge heart and also the struggle of the pain as well. I told her it was important to let that stuff out whether she runs around the yard and screams for a minute, draws (which is one of her favorite things to do) or talks to someone she can trust to not judge her. By holding that stuff in, it can take a toll on the body AND the mind and that trying to shut it down and keep it inside, she was not only blocking the pain but also the light and the joy that she has inside her.

Unfortunately most of us are not taught better ways of coping as we grow up and often are much older before we learn (if we do at all), but holding it in or putting up walls may seem to keep the darkness or pain at bay, but it also keeps the light and joy out. It saddened me a bit too that she has already learned that it is safer to shutdown than to be herself and share her heart. I personally believe that we are much better off with sweet, loving hearts like hers in the world and that we all would benefit by choosing to be courageous enough to share our own as well.

Just in those few moments after the tears began falling and her heart opened enough to share that one truth for her, there was a weight that lifted and I could see her energy lighten. I could see that she was still fighting back other things going on, but I reassured her that if she needed to talk more, I was available. This probably only took 15 minutes or less, but in that time, we both felt a connection and love that only compassion and understanding can bring. It was a gift we gave each other and I am so grateful.

In our world today, it takes a great deal of courage to be our true selves and to let others in. I believe it requires much more courage than continuing in our normal routines and habits that tend to make us feel unhappy or discontent, efforting to try *not* to feel because we don't have time or it won't fix anything. Those few moments remind me of how we both choose courage; to trust, to open, to be who we are and to love more, even when we are afraid of getting hurt. The only way to truly live a whole hearted life, is to open and take the leap.

There are no guarantees. More hurt may come as a result and yet when you truly let yourself be seen and loved and accepted regardless of your imperfections, the joy and connections you make, give you greater strength to be yourself and make your heart soar with a love that is exquisitely powerful. It is then, that we experience true peace within ourselves and begin to have the courage to also share the gift of living authentically with others.

I encourage each of you to take the time today to share your heart with someone you trust or just sit quietly and listen while another shares with you. You will find your heart overflowing with joy and contentment, just being you as well as offering another the feeling of being loved for who they are.

My passion for being of service stems from my own personal work and a calling from Spirit. It is this sense of purpose that drives me to show up and give of my heart in whatever way is needed. Living an Innergized life, for me means living from my heart, being authentic, truly listening to others, showing compassion and doing my own daily spiritual practice. These include meditation, prayer, reading, journaling, mindfulness practices, workshops etc.

I'm truly passionate about sharing what has worked for me and also guiding and encouraging others to find what works for them. Supporting each other through the ups and downs of life bring a sense of belonging, courage and love that ripples out to all those we touch. And that is how each one of us can truly make a difference!

Rev. Denise Judd: Unlocking the Heart

Rev. Denise Judd lives in St. Louis, Missouri with her young Australian Shepard, Echo. She currently works in the IT field and is also a speaker, teacher, counselor and writer of spiritual principles and practices focusing on compassion, meditation and mindfulness. It is her dream to begin writing and teaching full-time because that is what makes her heart soar, being of service and reminding others of their inherent beauty.

Her most recent projects are a 6-week class she created called, "What's Your Story" and her first novel which will be published in 2018.

"What's Your Story" helps participants become more aware of the "story" they have been living that impact their lives and relationships. The course allows for a greater understanding by delving deeper into the beliefs and patterns that have been automatic reactions and shifting them to conscious responses that create a life that an individual really wants.

Her first novel (with the working title: *Taking The Long Way Home – An inward journey from hopelessness to freedom*) is about a young girl who experiences trauma in childhood and in present day, does not want to continue living. She finds her way back to herself on a 30 day backpacking adventure with others who have experienced trauma by unlocking the pain and beliefs she has carried through life of being unworthy or unloved. Though the book is fiction, it has many spiritual principles that have guided Denise through her life and brought her to a place of living a whole-hearted life.

Continued...

She also enjoys occasionally posting a blog at https://connectourhearts.wordpress.com. Her website shares additional information and offers classes, meditations, coaching and an opportunity to contact her for speaking engagements.

Rev. Denise Judd
djudd0720@yahoo.com
www.DeniseJudd.com

https://twitter.com/connectourheart
https://www.instagram.com/revdj/
Personal Facebook: https://www.facebook.com/denise.judd.9
Fan page: https://www.facebook.com/connectourhearts/
Blog: https://connectourhearts.wordpress.com/

www.ingramcontent.com/pod-product-compliance
Lightning Source LLC
Chambersburg PA
CBHW052026290426
44112CB00014B/2403